THE COUNTER
REFORMATION

EDWARD MCNALL BURNS

Professor Emeritus of Political Science
Rutgers — The State University

72240

AN ANVIL ORIGINAL

under the general editorship of

LOUIS L. SNYDER

D. VAN NOSTRAND COMPANY, INC.

PRINCETON, NEW JERSEY

TORONTO   LONDON

NEW YORK

TO
ELMER DIEDRICH GRAPER
AND
ALFRED PROCTER JAMES
Inspiring teachers, wise and helpful counselors

D. VAN NOSTRAND COMPANY, INC.
120 Alexander St., Princeton, New Jersey (*Principal office*); 24 West 40 St., New York, N.Y.
D. VAN NOSTRAND COMPANY (Canada), LTD.
25 Hollinger Rd., Toronto 16, Canada
D. VAN NOSTRAND COMPANY, LTD.
358, Kensington High Street, London, W.14, England

PREFACE

The Reformation of the sixteenth century was a great revolution, as momentous in its effects as the French Revolution or the Russian Revolution of 1917. It marked not simply the disruption of the medieval Church, but the transformation of a whole complex of political, economic, and cultural institutions. In upheavals of this kind, ideas play a particularly important role. Men seek to justify or rationalize what they are doing, and the ideas thus generated provide the incitement for new and further actions. For this reason revolutions commonly follow a definite pattern or alternation of moderate and radical phases. After an initial stage of agitation for relatively moderate changes, the extremists take command, and the revolution swings into a violent or radical course. The early Protestants certainly did not intend that their doctrine of the priesthood of believers should be taken literally. But the Anabaptists did just that and construed it to mean that every man should really be his own priest, and that the professional clergy should be abolished.

Because of his conviction of the paramount importance of ideas the author has given a larger place to them than is commonly assigned in books of this kind. He has subordinated the narrative history in such a way as to give primary emphasis to the intellectual currents that were the germinating causes of most of the events. More than half of the excerpts chosen for Selected Readings have been taken from philosophical and theological writings, and only about one-third are political and ecclesiastical documents.

Because of his conception of the Reformation as an ideological revolution, the author has not always found it possible to separate clearly its Catholic and Protestant phases. Broadly speaking, both sprang from the same ferment of intellectual causes. Despite many salutary achievements, both were largely reactionary movements aimed at repudiating the present and turning the clock back to some more remote condition of faith and austerity. The Protestants were more resolute in this than the Catholics; yet both placed a premium on dogma and repression and scorned the intellectual and artistic advances of the Renaissance as heathen accomplishments. The developments in political theory give even more significant proof of the basic similarity of the two movements. Lutherans and Anglicans were just as vigorous in asserting the supremacy of the state over the Church as were the Catholic supporters of the kings of France. And it was not accidental that the teachings of radical Calvinists with regard to rebellion and tyrannicide were almost identical with those of the Jesuits.

EDWARD MCNALL BURNS

Santa Barbara, California

TABLE OF CONTENTS

PART II—SELECTED READINGS

Part I

THE COUNTER REFORMATION

— 1 —

THE MEANING AND NATURE
OF THE REFORMATION

Before undertaking the study of a subject, one must make sure that he understands its nature. The reader must not be baffled by loose usage of such terms as Reformation, Counter Reformation, Protestant Revolution, Renaissance in Religion, and so forth. More important, he must avoid thinking of the Reformation as a revolt of righteous and God-fearing theologians and their pious followers against a corrupt and tyrannical Church whose decadence could no longer be tolerated. He must realize that the sixteenth century, the age of the Reformation, was an age of upheaval much like the century in which he now lives. The foundations of an old society were crumbling, just as they seem to be today, and men were largely the instruments of forces more powerful than they. In a sense more real than we can easily imagine, an old world was dying and a new one was struggling to be born. Henry Charles Lea, a distinguished authority on church history, has said that the motives for the upheaval of the sixteenth century "were largely secular rather than spiritual." The religious changes incident to the Reformation "were not the object sought but the means for attaining the object." [1] The object sought was nothing less than the repudiation of the Middle Ages and the transition to a modern regime of nationalism, indi-

---

[1] *Cambridge Modern History* (New York: Macmillan Co., 1907), vol. I, p. 653.

vidualism, the sanctification of wealth, and the acceptance of all-powerful secular states.

Meaning of the Term "Reformation." The term "Reformation" is loosely used in a variety of ways. It is often employed as a synonym for the Protestant break with Catholicism in the sixteenth century. Such distinguished historians as James MacKinnon, Preserved Smith, James Harvey Robinson, Thomas M. Lindsay, and Henry S. Lucas were sometimes addicted to using it in this sense. Actually, the Reformation was a much broader movement. It included, of course, the Protestant rupture with Catholicism, which is more accurately called the Protestant Revolution. It included also a vigorous reform movement within the Catholic Church, which had antecedents extending far back into the Middle Ages, and which was only in a partial sense a reaction to the Protestant outbreak. The Reformation as a whole was not simply a religious movement, but had a political, social, and economic character as well. Indeed, in the opinion of some historians, the two major causes of its Protestant phase were the rise of a capitalist economy and the growth of nationalist resentment against domination by Rome. The Catholic reform movement, in the beginning at least, was almost exclusively religious in character, though its effects eventually overleaped the bounds of religion. Its primary objective was to purge the Church of corruption and bring it back to some pristine stage of purity. Later, as it fought to recover lost ground and to prevent further defections from its ranks, it extended its activities into education, politics, censorship, and persecution.

Meaning of the Term "Counter Reformation." The term "Counter Reformation" is now recognized by many historians as a misnomer, or at least as awkward and misleading. It implies that Catholic reform was limited to the period following the first stages of the Protestant Revolution, and that it was essentially a reaction against the Protestant outbreak. It gives little or no credit to the persistent efforts of pious Catholics to reform their own Church, both prior to and regardless of the incursions of Protestantism. Actually, such reform movements long antedated the Protestant Revolution. They included the Cluny movement of the tenth century, aimed at the reform of Benedictine monasticism and the eradication of such evils as *simony,* or the buying and selling of Church offices. They included also the Carthusian and Cistercian movements to set an example of purity and austerity for the regular clergy, and the Franciscan and Dominican movements to prod the Church into a more solicitous concern for the welfare of the entire society. They included the mystics and such pietists as the Brethren of the Common Life, the Beguines and Beghards, and the Friends of God —all of whom sought to make religion more personal and to diminish the importance of ecclesiastical machinery. Finally, they included the Church councils of the fourteenth and fifteenth centuries, whose efforts were directed toward making the Church more democratic, or at least more aristocratic and less monarchical than it had been since the time of Gregory VII. (*See Reading No. 5C.*)

The Renaissance and the Reformation. A common practice of many writers on the history of religion is to describe the Reformation as a kind of religious counterpart or offshoot of the Renaissance. For example, J. Addington Symonds referred to the Reformation as "the Teutonic Renaissance." [2] True, the two movements were closely related. Both were products of the resurgence of individualism that swept over Europe at the close of the Middle Ages. Both had a similar background of economic causes in the growth of capitalism and the rise of a bourgeois society. Both had roots in the development of nationalism, especially as it manifested itself in the ambitions of monarchs to gain control over religious as well as secular affairs within their kingdoms. Equally significant, though not so well recognized, was the fact that many of the humanists, particularly those in northern Europe, were just as much interested in reform of religion as they were in a return to the classics. This interest was notably characteristic of the English and Dutch humanists. It was characteristic to a

[2] "The Renaissance," *Encyclopaedia Britannica,* Eleventh Edition (New York: The Encyclopaedia Britannica Company, 1911), vol. XXIII, p. 89.

lesser extent of the French and German humanists. Rabelais
and Montaigne were too earthy and skeptical to care about
reform in religion except to alleviate intolerance and persecution. Johann Reuchlin and Crotus Rubianus, eminent
among German humanists, devoted themselves chiefly to
scholarly and contemplative pursuits. Though they satirized
the ignorance and greed of the clergy, they had no abiding
interest in changes in theology or in Church organization.
(*See Reading No. 1A.*) Their contemporary, Ulrich von
Hutten, was more fiery, but he was also more erratic. He
dedicated a large portion of his life to waging crusades on
behalf of German nationalism and the lesser nobility against
the powerful lords of the Empire. He was an embittered
rebel against almost every institution of the established
order and exerted some influence upon Luther.

But the spirit of the Renaissance was not the spirit of the
Reformation. The essence of the Renaissance as an intellectual and artistic movement was enjoyment of this life
and indifference to the supernatural. The spirit of the
Reformation was otherworldliness and contempt for the
things of the flesh as inferior to the spiritual. In the judgment of the humanist, man's nature was inherently good;
in the view of the reformer, whether Protestant or Catholic,
it was corrupt and depraved. The leaders of the Renaissance
believed in reason and tolerance; the followers of Luther,
Calvin, and Loyola emphasized faith and conformity. For
the humanist, forbearance and good will were cardinal
virtues, and education and persuasion the only legitimate
means of winning men over to new beliefs. For most of the
reformers, reason was "the Devil's mistress," and sword
and faggot the accepted instruments for enforcing uniformity of belief.

Instead of thinking of the Reformation as the Renaissance
in religion, one should reserve for that honor the so-called
Christian Renaissance initiated by the Brethren of the
Common Life and carried to its highest fulfillment in the
teachings of Sir Thomas More and Erasmus. Although the
Brethren of the Common Life were more deeply committed
to mysticism than they were to rationalism, they did believe
in the value of education and maintained one of the best

schools in Europe at Deventer, in the Low Countries. For the most part, the Brethren of the Common Life accepted medieval Christianity. They were not rebels or radical reformers. Their gospel, known as the *Devotio Moderna,* had as its principal objective a more personalized religion. Its prophets believed in cultivating the inner life, in imitating Christlike purity and simplicity, and in devoting their energies to helping the poor. In general, they raised no protest against either the dogmas or the observances of the Church. It was inevitable, however, that some of them should be affected by the more critical attitudes of humanism. The humanist demand for a return to the original sources led to a more careful study of the New Testament and to disturbing comparisons between medieval Christianity and the religion of the Gospels. One of the first to make such comparisons was Wessel Gansfort, a friend of Thomas à Kempis and a leading apostle of the *Devotio Moderna.* Though his works were not published until after the beginning of the Reformation, he anticipated some of the teachings of the Protestant Reformers. He questioned the need of confessing one's sins to a priest and vigorously criticized the system of indulgences. He taught that a person could be saved from his sins by sincere repentance and by a deep mystical love of the Savior. He exalted the authority of the Scriptures above that of the Popes and Church councils, and relegated the priesthood so far into the background as to make it unnecessary. Yet he was not a Protestant. He did not preach a new theology, nor did he advocate the overthrow of the Roman Church or the secession of his followers from it.

The ideals of the Christian Renaissance attained their broadest development in the work of John Colet (1367?-1519) and Sir Thomas More (1478-1535) in England and Desiderius Erasmus (1466?-1536) in the Low Countries. Colet was a humanist who became Dean of St. Paul's Cathedral in London. Though not much interested in theology, he won fame for his studies in the literal meaning of Biblical texts. He disapproved of auricular confession and celibacy of the clergy, but he seems not to have dreamed of a formal break with Catholicism. His friend and younger contemporary, Sir Thomas More, had a deeper interest in philosophy. Though most of his philosophy was political and social, it was his religious ideals that forced him to choose the supreme sacrifice of martyrdom. He was beheaded by Henry VIII in 1535 for refusing to acknowledge the English monarch as supreme head of the Church of England. Perhaps his punishment by Henry saved him from the infliction of a similar penalty by the Church of Rome; for More not only advocated religious toleration but advanced the philosophic conception that creeds are a matter of indifference. The religion described in his Utopia was essentially deistic. It consisted primarily of a simple public service in which worshipers of all shades of belief participated. Instead of demanding religious uniformity it openly encouraged disagreements. (*See Reading No. 1D.*)

The most distinguished leader of the Christian Renaissance was the Prince of the Humanists, Desiderius Erasmus. Though his mind was, of course, preoccupied with diverse philosophical and literary interests, he reserved not a little time and energy for religion. Like More, he could see no merit in the dogmatism and violence of the Protestant Revolution, but he went beyond More in attacking Catholic observances. He specifically condemned fasting, pilgrimages, the veneration of relics, the invocation of saints, and the sale of indulgences. Whereas More favored a kind of deism, Erasmus stressed the inwardness of religion. Piety, love, and devotion to the teachings and example of Jesus, rather than sacraments and ceremonies, constituted in his judgment the essence of Christianity. At the same time, he had no desire to separate religion from reason. He thought that Luther's attempt to place piety and reason in opposition could only prove detrimental to both. It was the constant ambition of the Prince of the Humanists to oppose irrationalism in all its forms and to propagate a religion of simple piety and rational conduct based upon what he called the "philosophy of Christ." Scarcely anything could be farther removed from the ferocious zeal of the Protestant Reformers than the Christian humanism of Erasmus. (*See Reading No. 1B.*) The superstitious extravagances of sixteenth-century Catholicism repelled him, but it was alien to his temper to lead a crusade against them. Convinced of the basic goodness of man, he believed that all misery and injustice would eventually disappear if the sunlight of reason could be allowed to penetrate the caverns of ignorance, credulity, and hate. With nothing of the fanatic about him, he stood for liberality of mind, for reasonableness and conciliation rather than for fierce intolerance of evil. He shrank from the violence and passion of war whether between nations, classes, or creeds. Though the Catholics of his time did not like him, he was nonetheless a discerning prophet of reform from within. Deference to his gospel might well have preserved the unity of the Church and averted much of the strife and oppression of the sixteenth and succeeding centuries. (*See Reading No. 1C.*)

— 2 —

FORERUNNERS OF THE
CATHOLIC REFORMATION

The Mystics. Mysticism is almost as old as religion itself. Indeed, it is difficult to conceive of religion without some element of the mystical in it. For the mystic emphasizes the indwelling presence of the divine in all things, and stresses the possibility of direct communion between man and his god and the ultimate and complete absorption of the human soul into the divine. But if mysticism is almost an essential component of religion it is at the same time a thorn in the side of organized religion. For mysticism seems to make the ministrations of a church unnecessary. Carried to its logical extreme, mysticism recognizes no need for the services of priests or for sacraments, lustrations, confessions, and sermons. The mystic really assumes that the individual can be his own priest, and that piety and contemplation are the only aids necessary for establishing a union between man and the divine. Nevertheless, the Catholic Church has always dealt very gently with its mystics, much more so than the leading Protestant denominations. Luther, for example, after the excesses of the Peasants' Revolt and especially of such leaders as Thomas Münzer, recognized mysticism as a dangerous, disintegrating force, even though he himself, at the beginning of his career, had been deeply influenced by such mystics as Meister Eckhart. The Roman Church, by contrast, has consistently revered its mystics and has canonized a great many of them. One has only to remember St. Bernard, St. Francis, St. Ignatius of Loyola, and St. Bonaventura to realize what a prominent place mystics

18

have occupied in the history of Catholicism. Even the most extreme and otherworldly of them—e.g., St. Teresa and St. Bernard—have received the same veneration as those who combined rational and practical interests with their devotion to the spiritual. The explanation may be found in the fact that most of the mystics were men and women so renowned for deeds of piety and charity that it would have been hazardous for the Church to disown or ignore them.

Mysticism reached a peak of intensity in the fourteenth and fifteenth centuries, especially in central Europe. The causes were twofold. The conflict between the rival emperors, Frederick of Austria and Louis of Bavaria, inflicted great hardship upon the people. To add to their miseries, the Black Death swept over Central Europe in 1348. In the midst of confusion and fear and a growing distrust of authority, men turned for support and comfort to an individualist type of religion. But their leaders were not revolutionists or rebels. They did not seek to overthrow the Church or to separate from it. They would have been satisfied merely with a less worldly and more spiritual religion within the framework of the existing institution. Though some of their influence contributed to the rise of Protestantism, this was an incidental and not an intentional result. The mystics were not Protestants and had little interest in the doctrinal issues that bulked so large in the thinking of Luther and Calvin.

The father of speculative mysticism in central Europe was Meister Eckhart (1260?-1327). Little is known of his life, but he was a native of western Germany who appears to have entered the Dominican order and to have served as a professor at one of the colleges in Paris. Later he repudiated the Aristotelianism of the Dominicans and adopted some of the premises and methods of the Neo-Platonists. He was a Christian pantheist, who taught that God and the spiritual universe are one, and that man's chief aim in life should be the reunion of his individual soul with the divine. This end he believed could be accomplished by intense contemplation and deep yearning. (*See Reading No. 2A.*)

Eckhart's chief disciples were Heinrich Suso (1300-1366)

and Johann Tauler (1300-1361). Suso's mysticism was
thoroughly medieval. He questioned no doctrines or ceremonies of the Church, but stressed the importance of winning personal salvation by extreme asceticism and the practice of good works. Johann Tauler was neither so emotional
as Suso nor so philosophical as Eckhart. He centered his
attention rather upon practical piety and service to his fel-
low men. When the Black Death came to his native city
of Strasbourg in 1348, he refused to flee but remained in
the city to encourage and help the terrorized and the
stricken. For some time he was associated with a mystical
and ascetic sect known as the Friends of God, who cultivated simplicity and equality as cardinal virtues and may
be regarded as spiritual ancestors of the Quakers. Unlike
some other mystics, Tauler denied that personal salvation
should be the chief aim of religion. He taught instead that
the real objective of Christian faith should be the love and
glorification of God. He is credited with having coined the
aphorism that a true Christian is one who would be willing
to be damned for the glory of God.

The most renowned of the pre-Reformation mystics was
undoubtedly Thomas à Kempis (c.1380-1471). Originally
known as Thomas Hammerken, he was a native of north-
western Germany. His mother was a teacher of small children, his father a poor, hard-working peasant. From child-
hood Thomas was shy and self-effacing, loving books and
quiet corners all his days. He received a good education in
the school of the Brethren of the Common Life at Deventer, but a conviction of sin and a vision of the anger
and forgiveness of the Virgin determined him upon a
monastic career. He took the vows of the Augustinian order
at the age of twenty-seven. Foremost among all the works
attributed to him was *The Imitation of Christ,* which remained the chief devotional book of pious Christians for
centuries. It has been translated into more languages than
any other book except the Bible. The *Imitation* reveals its
author as a humble, unquestioning Catholic who believes
with childlike simplicity in the dogmas and ritual of the
medieval Church. He asks for not a single change in the
system and invites no one to separate from it. All is per-

fect, and to win salvation the individual needs but to emulate the life of a medieval monk. The true religion is spiritual, and the morality necessary to accompany it consists of privation, humility, sacrifice, and suffering. The mysticism of Thomas à Kempis was more selfish and unsocial than that of some of his predecessors, of Johann Tauler, for instance. But possibly these qualities are what gave it its wide appeal. (*See Reading No. 2B.*)

The Unorthodox Sects and Religious Communities. Closely related to the example of individual mystics was the influence of various sects and religious communities that flourished without the official sanction of the Church. The oldest of these which may be considered as in some degree a protagonist of Catholic Reform was the Waldensian sect. The Waldensians or Waldensees, were followers of Peter Waldo, a rich merchant of Lyon who gave his wealth to the poor. He founded, in 1170, a lay order whose members held all their goods in common and devoted themselves to preaching and ministering to the needs of the less fortunate. Though Waldo had no intention of founding a sect outside the Church, he soon ran into conflict with the hierarchy on account of the privileges he claimed for his followers. The most offensive of these, apparently, was the privilege of preaching to all who would listen. This was a privilege which the Church regarded as reserved for the ordained clergy. Waldo also insisted upon using the Gospel in the vernacular languages instead of in Latin as desired by the Church. Some of Waldo's more radical followers appointed their own priests, taught that the sacraments were merely symbolical, and held that the ministrations of an immoral priest were invalid. Waldensians of this radical persuasion eventually formed their own church or were gathered up into the powerful current of Protestantism. The main body of them never separated from Catholicism but remained loyal to it, hoping by zealous efforts and a good example to purge it of worldliness, self-seeking, and corruption.

The pre-Reformation sects of greatest importance, though, were undoubtedly those of the fourteenth and fifteenth centuries. Pre-eminent among them was the Brethren of the Common Life, founded by Gerhard Groote about 1370. The Brethren composed an order of laymen living according to a rule and devoting themselves to practical piety and education of the young. Their school at Deventer was one of the best in Europe. Its peak enrollment of over 2000 included numerous young men who later gained fame as foremost humanists of the Northern Renaissance. Included also were such religious leaders as Thomas à Kempis and Wessel Gansfort. The Christianity of the Brethren was based not upon the Scholastic philosophy or the doctrines of the medieval theologians but upon the teachings of Jesus. It sought to inculcate a piety founded upon simple faith and deeds of charity and mercy for the benefit of the unfortunate. It minimized the importance of theology, ecclesiastical organization, sacraments, and ceremonies. In short, it relegated to the background nearly the whole system of medieval Christianity, with its doctrines and observances and its elaborate machinery for defining and maintaining them. But this movement was not a religious revolution, and it was not Protestantism. Its leaders had no desire for a violent rupture with Catholicism, and few of them became Protestants. Their aim was to accomplish the reform of religion by education, example, and gentle persuasion. They occasionally lent themselves to satire, but nothing more violent. Their purposes were epitomized by Erasmus, not by Luther or Calvin.

Still other organizations embodying the spirit of religious reform in the fourteenth and fifteenth centuries were the Brethren of the Free Spirit and the Friends of God. They seemed to differ mainly in the geographic localities in which they flourished. The Brethren of the Free Spirit were concentrated in the Lower Rhine Valley and the Friends of God in the Upper Valley, including western Switzerland. Both were lay orders and cultivated a mystical approach to religion. They scoffed at Popes and Church councils and taught the reality of direct communication between man and God. They preached no revolt against the Church, however, but simply reform from within. They were partners in a great movement that had begun as far back as the twelfth century. The Waldenses were its prime initiators. They were soon followed by the Beghards and Beguines in southern France, the Rhineland, and the Low Countries. The Beghards were men, the Beguines women. Both were groups of humble folk who lived according to a rule and practiced poverty. Caring little about creeds and doctrines, they devoted themselves to welfare work among the poor. The Beghards, however, adopted some of the heretical teachings of Peter Waldo, especially the right of unordained but pious individuals to preach the Gospel. Both movements were vehicles of gentle protest against a religion that was steeped in worldly and political concerns and had almost forgotten the precepts of its Founder.

It is tempting to include as forerunners of the Catholic Reformation the followers of John Wycliffe and John Hus. Both, in fact, agreed with many of the teachings of their predecessors since the time of Peter Waldo. They condemned the possession of property by the clergy, exalted the Scriptures above the teachings of the Church and its Fathers, and taught the direct dependence of the individual upon God and the right of every man to be his own priest. But they were more radical than most of their predecessors in condemning the medieval Christian system. They considered the Church to be composed of those predestined to be saved and regarded the hierarchy headed by the Pope as spurious and unnecessary. They attacked all seven of the sacraments, with the exception of marriage; while Wycliffe, at least, rejected transubstantiation (or the doctrine of the miraculous conversion of the bread and wine of the Eucharist [Mass] into the body and blood of Christ). Pilgrimages, the invocation of saints, indulgences, and the veneration of relics also came under their ban. With their repudiation of the externals of religion and their emphasis on the supremacy of the Scriptures and predestination, they belong in the current of ideas and attitudes that led to Protestantism rather than to Catholic Reform. (*See Readings Nos. 3A and B.*)

The Conciliar Movement. One other movement, however, does deserve a place among the forerunners of the Catholic Reformation, even though its efforts were largely a failure. This was the Conciliar movement, which

gathered momentum and gave great promise during the
fifteenth century. The Conciliar movement was predicated
upon the doctrine that the supreme authority in the Church
should be not the Pope but a general council representing
the whole body of believers. The papacy, they taught, has
no inherent power but is a creature of the Church and
should therefore be under the control of its representatives.
The latter can depose a tyrannical or unworthy Pope and
set up another in his place. The leaders of the Conciliar
movement argued that absolute monarchy was obsolete,
and they could cite as evidence the establishment of Parliament in England and the Estates-General in France.

The most distinguished leaders of the Conciliar movement were John Gerson, Chancellor of the University of
Paris, and Nicholas of Cusa, an eminent scientist and
philosopher as well as theologian. As a philosopher, Gerson belonged to the radical school of Nominalists who
opposed the rationalism and Aristotelianism of the Scholastics. But instead of substituting science for metaphysics,
Gerson embraced mysticism. He was not a radical reformer, much less a revolutionist, but rather a compro-
miser and an opportunist. He eventually repudiated most
of the "liberalism" of his earlier career and dedicated himself to the writing of mystical and devotional tracts. It is
ironical that at the Council of Constance he acted as chief
prosecutor of John Hus.

The philosophy of John Gerson rested squarely upon the
dogma that the unity of the Church was a supremely important consideration. (*See Reading No. 5A.*) Without
unity it could not remain the true Church. When this unity
was broken, as it had been during the Great Schism (1378-
1417), it could only be repaired by the whole body of
believers. The papacy obviously could not do it, since
there were now two Popes, one at Rome and another at
Avignon, each loudly proclaiming himself the rightful successor of the Apostle Peter. But in order to restore unity
the Church Council must be considered to possess supreme
authority. It must have power to ensure its own continuance, to correct abuses within the Church, and to suppress

or depose its tyrannical officials. Popes and other members of the hierarchy were not the rulers of the Church, but its agents. Here Gerson and his followers fell back upon an ancient medieval theory which held that every government must be a government of laws. These laws were not the statutes or decrees of a parliament or king but the aggregate of customs and practices generally accepted as valid. Determination of which rules had this general acceptance was the function of the chief men of the realm or society. In the case of the Church this function should be exercised by a church council, composed of representatives of the whole body of believers or, at least, of the clergy. Like all medievalists, Gerson looked to the traditions and observances of the past as the best safeguards of the rights of the citizen. Not what the community might desire for the future but what had the sanction of long history was his measure of good government.

A broader minded if not more consistent exponent of Conciliar theory was Nicholas Cusanus or Nicholas of Cusa. The son of a poor fisherman of the Rhine Valley, he was sent by his employer, the Count of Manderscheid, to the school of the Brethren of the Common Life at Deventer and afterwards to the University of Padua. Disillusioned with the practice of law, he entered the priesthood and rose to be Archdeacon of Liége. As a member of the Council of Basel, he prepared and read a work entitled *On Catholic Harmony,* in which he asserted the supremacy of councils over Popes and attacked the authenticity of the Isidorean Decretals and the Donation of Constantine. A few years later, however, he reversed his attitude and became a stanch defender of the supremacy of the Pope. In 1448 he was made a Cardinal by Pope Nicholas V. Like Gerson, Cusanus also rejected the Aristotelian rationalism of the Scholastics. He substituted for it a kind of mystical pantheism with God as "the absolute maximum and absolute minimum" who can be apprehended only by intuition and includes all that is or ever can be. More significant were his contributions to science. He worked out a plan for calendar reform that anticipated the one put into effect by

Pope Gregory XIII in 1582. He also anticipated Copernicus in developing a theory of the rotation of the earth around the sun.

For Nicholas of Cusa the supreme desideratum of Christian society was harmony. Without harmony a Christian society would be impossible, for brotherhood was the essence of Christian living. The key to harmony Nicholas found in the divine origin of all things. From this viewpoint state and church formed an integral organic unity. Neither was the superior of the other, and no natural enmity existed between them. But if, in the ultimate sense, all power is derived from God, in the immediate sense it springs from man. The source of Papal authority, for instance, is the consent and agreement of the Christian community. In no lesser degree the authority of the Emperor comes from the people whom he governs. Both Pope and Emperor should be subject to a representative council capable of giving advice as to the rights of the people defined in ancient custom and in natural law. Defiance of such advice by either monarch would justify his deposition by the council.

At the peak of his career Nicholas of Cusa may be regarded, with some warrant, as one of the great liberals of history. He seems to have doubted the effectiveness of persecution and exhibited some sympathy for religious toleration. More important, he carried forward some of the great traditions of the Middle Ages which helped to lay the foundations of modern democratic theory. He rejected both Papal and secular absolutism and taught that the source of earthly authority is the consent of the governed. He revived the Stoic theory of natural law and natural rights which had been generally accepted by medieval philosophers but which was in danger of being undermined by royal and imperial apologists like Pierre Dubois and Marsiglio of Padua.

Aside from the theoretical contributions of John Gerson and Nicholas of Cusa, the Conciliar movement was largely a failure. No significant reforms emerged from it, and the efforts of its leaders to democratize the Church were nullified by the Popes. (*See Reading No. 5B.*) Three great councils were actually held, but their accomplishments in line with the purposes of the movement were almost negligible. The Council of Pisa, convoked in 1409, was worse than a failure. It attempted to heal the Great Schism by summoning the two Popes before it. When they failed to appear they were declared "contumacious" and deposed. The Council then proceeded to elect a new Pope. For a time it appeared that this action might solve the problem. But the deposed Popes excommunicated the Council, and Christendom was left with three Popes, each claiming to be Christ's vicar on earth.

The Council of Pisa was followed by the Council of Constance in 1414-1418. The latter was a magnificent assemblage comprising twenty-nine cardinals, nearly 200 archbishops and bishops, and scores of lesser clergy, secular princes, and representatives of the universities. Their first action, taken in deference to the Emperor Sigismund, was to proceed against the Hussite heresy. The noted heretic was summoned before the Council, convicted, and sentenced to be burned. The Council then turned its attention to the issue of Church sovereignty. Two decrees were issued, *Sacrosanct* and *Frequens*. The first, issued in 1415, proclaimed that the general council had its authority "immediately from Christ," and that everyone, even the Pope, was bound to obey it in matters pertaining to the faith, the preservation of unity, and the "reformation of the Church of God in head and members." (*See Reading No. 5C.*) The decree *Frequens,* issued in 1417, declared the frequent holding of church councils to be "one of the chief means of cultivating the Lord's field." The decree provided, therefore, that a new council should be held every ten years at a place agreed upon one month before the conclusion of the preceding council. (*See Reading No. 5E.*) The council would then become a kind of continuing authority in the Church. At least, there would always be one actively functioning or being awaited at the end of a definite period.

Late in 1417 a conclave of the Council of Constance elected a member of the respected family of Colonna as Pope Martin V. Because he was a good and gentle man, free from intrigue, he was gradually accepted by all fac-

tions. Europe, moreover, was tired of schismatics, and conflicts among the various nations made further achievements by the Council impossible. Accordingly, no one shed
any tears when Pope Martin dissolved it in 1418 and summoned a new council to meet in Pavia in 1423. Neither
the Council of Pavia nor its successor, the Council of
Siena, accomplished anything and both were dissolved by
Papal action. No further councils would probably have
been held had not the Hussite heresy still constituted a
grave threat. Hus himself had been burned by order of the
Council of Constance, but his ideas had not been eradi-
cated. They continued to be preached in the Bohemian
province of the Empire by a sect known as Taborites. Combined with Bohemian nationalism, and with social and economic radicalism, their activities posed a challenge to the
rule of the German aristocracy. Since the confederate structure of the Empire prevented the raising of an efficient
army, some German princes demanded that the Pope summon a council. The Holy Father, who was now Eugenius
IV, would have preferred a crusade to exterminate the
Taborites, but he found little in the military situation of
Europe to inspire confidence in its success. He therefore
turned to a council as the logical alternative.

The Council of Basel was convoked in 1431. Almost immediately a conflict developed between the chief delegates
and the Pope. In desperation the Pope ordered its dissolu-
tion, but it refused to obey, and finally retaliated by re-
affirming the decree *Sacrosanct* adopted at the Council of
Constance. To supplement this action a new decree was
issued providing that each newly elected Pope must take
an oath declaring that councils were superior to Popes.

Nevertheless, it was the papacy that finally gathered the
garlands of victory. Eugenius IV, in return for implicit
promises to aid the Greeks against the Turks, was able to
obtain from the Greek church an acknowledgment of his
headship of Christendom. Although the delegates at Basel
ordered his deposition, the prestige of the Council declined
while that of the papacy increased. The climax came in
1460 when Pope Pius II issued the bull *Execrabilis*. In it
he condemned appeals to Church councils against the Pope

as "an execrable abuse." He declared that anyone resorting to such appeals would *"ipso facto* incur sentence of excommunication,"* from which he could not be absolved except by the Roman pontiff "and when at the point of death." (*See Reading No. 5D.*) The bull *Execrabilis* dealt a death blow to the theories of conciliar supremacy enunciated in the decrees *Sacrosanct* and *Frequens.*

How can the failure of the Conciliar movement be explained? For one thing, it was a result of discord among the exponents of the Conciliar theories. Some wished to give the highest priority to the correction of abuses within the Church. Others, largely indifferent to reform, emphasized primarily the maintenance of orthodoxy against the Hussites and other heretics. Conflicts also developed between higher and lower clergy, while nationalist jealousies precluded harmony between Germans and Italians and Italians and Frenchmen. Most important of all was the growth of political autocracy as a threat to the unity of the Church. Powerful kings, especially in France and England, aspired to make their absolutism complete by establishing their own national churches independent of the See of Rome. Many Europeans came to believe that the only way to prevent Christianity from being torn asunder was to rally behind the Bishop of Rome as the only rightful shepherd of the Christian flock. Popes, of course, were not loath to cultivate this sentiment and to use it in every way possible to strengthen their own position against the councils.

The failure of the Conciliar movement was one of the tragedies of history. Had it succeeded, it might well have exerted a decisive influence in preventing the growth of absolutism in both church and state. It would not necessarily have transformed the Church into a democracy, in the sense of the sovereignty of the majority, but in the words of J. N. Figgis, it would at least have made it a limited monarchy in which the danger of tyranny would be removed "by the power of a small body of permanent advisers, a continued council, and ultimately checked by a large representative assembly." [3] Despite the victory of

[3] *Studies of Political Thought from Gerson to Grotius* (Cambridge: Cambridge University Press, 1931), p. 44.

the Popes, the Conciliar movement nurtured the delicate plant of medieval constitutionalism and thereby contributed an important element to the crusade for limited government in the seventeenth and eighteenth centuries. But a long night of political absolutism delayed the triumph of this crusade.

— 3 —

BEGINNINGS OF THE
CATHOLIC REFORMATION

The Reform Movement in Spain. That the Catholic
Reformation should have begun in Spain, in the late fifteenth century, seems almost a paradox. The days of Spain's
greatness were still in the future. Cervantes, Lope de Vega,
El Greco, and Velasquez were not yet born. The liberal-
izing currents of Italian and French humanism were yet to
make their way to the Iberian peninsula. In 1479 the Inquisition was established at Seville, under the infamous Torquemada, and Spain became the arena of the most savage
persecution in Europe. It was directed primarily against
the Moors and the Jews. In January 1492, the last great
stronghold of the Moors, Granada, was captured, and three
months later the Jews were expelled from the country. It
is estimated that Spain lost 800,000 to 1,700,000 of her
most capable and prosperous citizens. These conquests and
expulsions were nothing less than disastrous to the cultural
and economic life of the nation. Yet they were at least
conducive to religious reform. In order to succeed in its
great crusade against unbelievers, Spanish Christianity
needed to be made as strong as possible by the elimination
of incompetence, sloth, and corruption.

The principal instigator of religious reform in Spain was
Francisco Ximenes de Cisneros (1436-1517), an austere
and pious member of the Franciscan order. Of lowly origin, he became a zealous defender of the monarchy against
the feudal aristocracy. In 1492 he was appointed Queen
Isabella's confessor and three years later Archbishop of
Toledo. He also served for a period as Inquisitor-General

and, like Torquemada, insisted upon ruthless treatment of Moors and Jews. In 1507 he became Cardinal Ximenes. One of the few Spanish churchmen to recognize the value of Renaissance culture, he did not hesitate to use the methods of pagan scholarship to advance the interests of the Christian religion. He appointed men of learning to high positions in the Church, but he imposed upon them a stringent morality and insisted that the members of his own order live in Franciscan poverty. He founded schools, including a great university at Alcalá, and sponsored and financed a translation of the Bible into four languages. Though his high positions required him to live in considerable opulence, in his private life he continued the rigorous asceticism that had characterized his early career as a Franciscan monk.

The work of Cardinal Ximenes was not the totality of Catholic reform in Spain. Other leaders, of course, were also active. Well known among them was Juan de Valdés (1500?-1541), who had come under the influence of both mysticism and the humanism of Erasmus. Though he severely criticized abuses in the Church, he contended that he was mainly interested in reforming the individual rather than institutions. Like Erasmus he urged a return to the "philosophy of Christ." Of some influence also was Juan de Vives (1492-1540), although he spent most of his creative life in Louvain, Oxford, and Bruges. Inspired by Erasmus he wrote treatises against Scholasticism and the excessive dependence of theologians upon ancient authority. His most important work was *On the Cause of Corruption of the Arts*, which is sometimes ranked with Sir Francis Bacon's *Novum Organum*.

The Catholic Reformation in Spain had early manifestations in other directions. One of these was asceticism, both collective and individual. It is estimated that by the end of the seventeenth century the peninsula contained more than 9,000 monasteries. Monks constituted nearly a fourth of the population, and about half of the land was in the possession of the orders. While Spanish monasticism received a primary impetus from the Brethren of the Common Life, it developed extremes of mysticism and asceticism that had never been characteristic of its Dutch and German predecessors.

The most noted of the individual Spanish ascetics was St. Teresa of Jesus (1515-1582), as she called herself. (*See Reading No. 2C.*) While still a child she contemplated sacrificing her life in the crusade against the Moors. At the age of eighteen she entered the Carmelite order and took the vows of a nun. When she was approaching forty she began to see visions and to experience trances or emotional seizures that were considered by her admirers as evidence of divine communication. In one of them the cross of her rosary was snatched from her hand. When returned it was made of jewels more brilliant than diamonds, visible only to her. Convinced that the troubles of the Church and the defections from it were the result of lax discipline in the monasteries, she determined to found a new order with a rule of unexampled severity. She obtained permission from the Pope to establish the Barefoot Carmelites, whose members would wear no shoes but sandals of rope, eat no meat, endure strict confinement to the cloister, and live on alms. Before she died in 1582 she had founded thirty units of the new order. When her tomb was opened nine months after her death, her flesh was said to be uncorrupted. A severed hand was reputed to perform miracles. Disinterred a second time to be buried in a more magnificent coffin, her body was mutilated further by superstitious relic-seekers.

After some years a reaction set in in Spain against mysticism and extreme asceticism. Melchior Cano, a Dominican theologian who died in 1560, founded a new Scholasticism and attempted to lead the Church back to the religious rationalism of St. Thomas Aquinas. The chief center of the movement was the University of Salamanca in north central Spain. For a season it gave promise of success, but the inability of its founder to tolerate the opinions of his rivals and his attempts to make the Spanish Church largely independent of Rome aroused the opposition of the papacy. Pope Paul IV denounced Cano as "a son of perdition." Eventually, the movement was engulfed by the rising tide of Jesuitism.

Early Reforms in Italy. The chief center of the Catholic Reformation was, of course, Italy. The Italian movement did not begin so early as did that in Spain, but it attained a more vigorous growth. To some extent, it was motivated by its Spanish precursor. Two of its chief instruments, the Inquisition and the Jesuit order, were of Spanish origin. In the main, however, the causes were indigenous to Italy. That country was the scene of the most flagrant corruption in the Church. In Italy the worldliness and power-seeking of the Renaissance Popes were most clearly evident. In addition, the invasion of Italy by Charles VIII of France in 1493-1495 and the sack of Rome by armies of the Emperor Charles V in 1527 convinced many people that even greater disasters would befall in the future unless the Church were reconstituted on a sounder moral and spiritual basis.

The Oratory of Divine Love. Internal reform of the Church in Italy, and in some other countries, was initiated largely by new religious societies and orders. First among them was the Oratory of Divine Love, a pious sodality founded in 1517. Its leaders were principally bishops and cardinals, though some eminent laymen were also included. Started in the vicinity of Rome, it spread throughout the peninsula. Since some of the original leaders had been infected with such Lutheran doctrines as justification by faith alone, the order aroused the hostility of the hierarchy, and in 1530 Pope Clement VII denounced it as heretical. His successor, Paul III, however, recognized its value to the Church and took it under his protection. He instructed a number of the leaders to draw up a *Consilium . . . de emendanda ecclesia,* or plan for reform of the Church. Completed in 1538, it called for strict observance of the laws of the Church, regulation of the distribution of benefices and dispensations, and suppression of scandalous conduct in religious houses and among the clergy.

The Theatine Order. Although the Oratorians suffered a deadly blow from the sack of Rome by the armies of Charles V in 1527, other societies soon appeared to supplement and continue their work. One was the Theatine

Order founded by Gaetano di Tiene, a noble of Vicenza. He had a worthy collaborator in Gian Pietro Caraffa, Archbishop of Brindisi. The plan of the Theatine founders was for an order of priests who would live in accordance with a rule and practice austerities after the fashion of monks. They were not even permitted to beg for alms but must support themselves out of their own funds or await the gifts of the pious. They anticipated the Jesuits in combining work in the world with the requirements of the monastic life. Like the Jesuits also they extended their activities into various countries. Their main theater of action was Italy, but they had additional centers in Spain, Portugal, Poland, Germany, and France.

The Capuchins. The most spectacular of the new orders founded in Italy was the Capuchin, or reformed Franciscan, order. The objective of its founder, Matteo da Boscio, was to return to the observances of St. Francis. In token thereof he adopted the pointed hood, or capuche, of the great leader of the Friars Minor. Like the Theatines, the Capuchins resolved to live in the world but not to succumb to its influences. Their aim was to serve the unfortunate and to set an example of piety and austerity to the faithful. They were probably the most democratic of the new orders. They not only preached to the masses but sought to place themselves on a plane of equality with them or even to descend a bit lower. Though the faith of the majority was unquestioning, opposition to the worldliness and wealth of the Church led in a few cases to sympathy with new doctrines. The third Vicar-General of the order, for instance, Bernardo Ochino, fell under the influence of Protestantism and fled to northern Europe. He finally became a pastor in Zürich, but was exiled to Poland as a Unitarian.

Founding of the Society of Jesus. The most active and influential of all the new orders participating in the Catholic Reformation was, of course, the Society, or Company, of Jesus. Established originally in Paris, it extended its activities into most other countries of Europe and eventually into the Americas and the Far East. Its founder was Ignatius of Loyola, a Spanish nobleman from the Basque country. His early career seems not to have differed much from that of other Spaniards of his class—a life of philandering and marauding as a soldier of the king. But about the time the Protestant Revolution was getting well under way in Germany, he was painfully wounded in a battle with the French. Multiple fractures in one of his legs required him to be hospitalized for many weeks. To pass the time he turned to reading, but he found nothing available except lives of the saints and a *Life of Christ* by Ludolf of Saxony. Realizing that the previous chapters of his own life were closed, he resolved to become a soldier of Christ. He decided that his first step should be a pilgrimage to Jerusalem, but an outbreak of the plague forced him to postpone the venture. He spent the next six months in acts of penance, soul-searching, meditation, and prayer. At length he found peace by writing down his inner experiences in his *Spiritual Exercises*. In its final form it was not a theological work but a book of discipline. It was intended to provide a set of instructions whereby the individual could control his will and emotions and subordinate his fleshly desires to the needs of the spirit. These ends were to be achieved, however, not with a view primarily to the salvation of one's soul but for the purpose of more effectively serving the Church. The *Spiritual Exercises* was essentially a handbook for the Christian knight rather than a manual of private devotions. (*See Reading No. 4A.*)

Early in 1523 Loyola set out for Palestine with the hope of converting the Moslems to Christianity. Soon he came to the conclusion that his efforts would be fruitless unless he improved his education. Accordingly, he returned and enrolled, at the age of thirty, in a preparatory school in Barcelona. Later he studied at the universities of Alcalá and Salamanca and finally at the University of Paris. In Paris he gathered about him a handful of admirers and faithful disciples. They dedicated themselves to the service of God, took vows of poverty and chastity, and pledged themselves to do missionary work among the Moslems after finishing their education. In 1537 Loyola and ten of his followers prepared for a new expedition to Palestine.

Unable to obtain passage because of a war between Venice and the Turks, they decided to make Rome "their Jerusalem." Calling themselves the Society of Jesus, they enlisted in the service of the Pope, promising to accept his authority and to obey his commands in whatever mission he might ordain for them. In 1540 their organization was approved by Pope Paul III. From then on it grew rapidly. When Loyola died in 1556, it could boast of a membership of about 1500.

Nature and Activities of the Jesuit Order. The Society of Jesus was by far the most militant of the religious orders fostered by the reforming zeal of the sixteenth century. It was not merely a monastic society but a company of soldiers sworn to defend the faith. Their weapons were not to be bullets and spears but eloquence, argumentation, instruction in the correct doctrines, and, if necessary, more worldly methods of exerting influence. The organization was patterned after that of a military company, with a General as commander-in-chief and an iron discipline enforced on the members. All individuality was suppressed, and a soldierlike obedience to the General was exacted of the rank and file. Only the highest of the four classes of members had any share in the government of the order. This little group, known as the Professed of the Four Vows, elected the General for life and consulted with him on important matters. But like all the others, they were bound to implicit obedience.

The activities of the Jesuits were numerous and varied. As indicated already, they conceived of themselves as the defenders of true religion. For this object they obtained authority from the Pope to hear confessions and grant absolution. Many of them became priests in order to gain access to the pulpit and expound the truth as the oracles of God. Still others served as agents of the Inquisition in the relentless war against heresy. In all of this work they followed the leadership of Mother Church as their infallible guide. They raised no questions and attempted to solve no mysteries. Loyola taught that if the Church should rule that white was black, it would be the duty of her sons to believe it. But the Jesuits were not satisfied merely to hold the field against the attacks of Protestants and heretics; they were ambitious to propagate the faith in the farthest corners of the earth—to make Catholics out of Buddhists, Moslems, the Parsees of India, and the untutored savages of the newly discovered continents. Before the Reformation had ended there were Jesuit missionaries in Africa, in Japan and China, and in North and South America. The most redoubtable of them was Francis Xavier (1506-1552), who was credited with having converted to Christianity hundreds of thousands of natives of India, Ceylon, Malaya, China, and Japan. Apparently, many of his conversions were quite superficial, since he considered willingness to submit to baptism the equivalent of an understanding acceptance of a new religion.

Jesuit Education. Yet another activity of the Jesuits was education. In some respects this activity outranked all the others. Unlike some of the founders of other orders, Loyola and his followers were not content with winning the masses but recognized the necessity of convincing the intellectual classes of Europe. To this end they established seminaries and colleges which rapidly became famous for the thoroughness if not the depth of their instruction in philosophy and theology, in mathematics and the classics, and eventually in some of the new sciences. The principal area of their educational activity was Germany, since they ardently hoped to win that country back from its Protestant apostasy. Loyola himself founded a German college as well as a Roman college. Under his immediate successors others were established at Cologne, Mayence, Munich, Trier, Augsburg, and Würzburg. It is noteworthy that the curriculum in these institutions resembled more closely that developed by Renaissance humanists than it did the curriculum of the medieval universities. It emphasized the classics and mathematics, slighted the Scholastic philosophy, and largely ignored the *trivium* (grammar, dialectic, and rhetoric) and *quadrivium* (arithmetic, geometry, music, and astronomy).

The most active exponent of Jesuit education was Peter Kanis or Canisius (1521-1597). He was born in the Low Countries, educated at Louvain and Cologne, and admitted to the Jesuit order in 1543. His first great enterprise was to combat Protestantism in Cologne where the loyalty of the Archbishop to the faith was definitely wavering. To facilitate the success of his venture Canisius founded a college in Cologne. Soon afterward he was sent by the Pope to teach in the University of Ingolstadt in Bavaria in the hope of saving that country for Catholicism. Though he was singularly successful in Bavaria and rose to the rectorship at Ingolstadt, Loyola ordered him in 1550 to go to Vienna where the task of combating heresy seemed even more formidable. In Vienna he preached before the court of King Ferdinand and became Dean of the Faculty of Theology at the University. While in Vienna he visited Poland and established colleges there. In 1556 he was appointed Provincial of Upper Germany, a region that included the hereditary domains of the Hapsburgs, with Bavaria, Swabia, and Switzerland.

Canisius' most notable contribution to the Catholic revival was the composition of his Catechisms. These included a *Catechismus minimus,* with 59 Questions and Answers; a *Catechismus minor,* with 102 Questions and Answers; and a *Catechismus major,* with 211 Questions and Answers. The *Catechismus minimus* was intended for children and uneducated people, while the *Catechismus major* was designed for students in the colleges and universities. The publication of these Catechisms tended to standardize Catholic doctrine, which in Germany at that time was in a fluid condition. They contributed not a little toward the maintenance and recovery of the Catholic faith not only in southern and western Germany but in Austria, Poland, Bohemia, and the Catholic cantons of Switzerland.

— 4 —

THE REFORM POPES

The success of the Catholic Reformation in accomplishing what it did required the leadership of some of the most noted Popes in the history of the Church. They alone could provide this leadership since the failure of the Conciliar movement had left the Church council in a distinctly subordinate position. Moreover, the Sacred College of Cardinals had had its status compromised by the fact that several of its members had taken a prominent part in the Conciliar movement and had been hopelessly divided during the period of the Great Schism. By the beginning of the sixteenth century, the unity of the Church had come to be identified exclusively with the papacy.

Adrian VI. The first in chronological order among the Reform Popes, though by no means the greatest, was Adrian VI of Utrecht (1522-1523). The first non-Italian Pope in 144 years and the last in history, he was apparently chosen to refute the criticism that the papacy was essentially an Italian institution. He had been associated with Cardinal Ximenes in Spain and had served as Inquisitor-General of Aragon. As Pope, Adrian made earnest attempts to limit the sale of indulgences and to reduce the number of matrimonial dispensations. His reform activities, however, had little effect, partly because his pontificate was too short but also because his austere and phlegmatic personality repelled many of his subordinates. The Italians regarded him as a pedantic moralist who was too stingy and mean-spirited to allow members of his court to indulge their appreciation of the beauty of classical antiquity.

Clement VII. Following the death of Adrian VI in 1523 the Cardinals returned to their old policy of electing a good-natured humanist or politician to the Fisherman's Throne. Their selection fell upon Giulio de Medici who took the name of Clement VII. He was a cousin of Pope Leo X, who had made him a Cardinal. Left an orphan soon after his birth, he was taken into the house of Lorenzo the Magnificent, who provided for his education. Personally free from the grosser vices, he was tolerant of the vices of others and had no interest in reform. A patron of literature and the arts, he neither understood Lutheranism nor recognized the gravity of its threat to the Church. The main cause of his troubles, however, was his weak and ineffective diplomacy. He allowed himself to become involved in the rivalry of King Francis I of France and Charles V, Holy Roman Emperor. The former, who did not take his religion seriously, pursued Machiavellian policies whenever they seemed likely to serve his own interests. As an exponent of the balance of power, he formed alliances with Protestant princes and even with Moslems to check the might of the Empire. Charles, conceiving himself as the ruler of a medieval Empire in association with a medieval Church, could brook neither the ambition of national monarchs nor the threat to universalism inherent in the Protestant Revolt. Though, as a Cardinal, Clement had supported Charles, after his election to the papacy he went over to the side of Francis. He seemed to think that the latter was the more powerful of the two, and that he would easily defeat the Imperial armies. It was a bad error of judgment. When the Pope entered into a formal alliance with Francis after having signed a treaty of submission with the Emperor, Charles invaded Italy. The result was the sack of Rome in May 1527 and the extinction of much of Renaissance culture in a horror of fire and blood. The Pope was besieged in the castle of St. Angelo and obliged to ransom himself with a payment of about $400,000. He was not released until the following November when he promised to call a general council to deal with Lutheranism.

Paul III. The first of the Popes to play a major role

in the Catholic Reformation was Paul III (1534-1549).
His predecessors for more than fifty years had been occupied almost entirely with secular interests. The one exception was Adrian VI, but his reign was too short to be
significant. Paul III was originally Alexander Farnese, a
member of a prominent Florentine family. Like Clement
VII, he obtained his education in the house of Lorenzo
the Magnificent. Papal preferment came to him at an early
age. To a liaison between his sister and Pope Alexander
VI he owed his Cardinal's hat, conferred when he was
not even a priest. He acquired so much power and privilege
during the reign of Leo X that he became a wealthy man.
Under Clement VII he occupied the most influential and
prominent place in the papal *Curia*. His election to the
papacy to succeed Clement in 1534 was virtually without
opposition.

The pontificate of Paul III was a major epoch in the
history of the Roman Church. Had conditions in Europe
been stable, the new Pope would probably have continued
the pleasure- and power-loving habits of most of his immediate predecessors. Like them, he practiced nepotism,
appointing his immediate relatives, including his illegitimate sons, to choice positions. Like his predecessors also,
he subsidized culture and patronized men of genius. He
began the Farnese Palace and commissioned Michelangelo
to paint *The Last Judgment* and resume work in designing
St. Peter's Church. But the age was turbulent and revo-
lutionary. By 1534 Protestantism had rent Christendom
asunder. England, the Scandinavian countries and large
portions of Germany, the Low Countries, and Switzerland
had already repudiated their allegiance to the See of Rome.
The King of France and some lesser monarchs were chal-
lenging political universalism, while even His Most Catholic
Majesty Charles V was threatening the independence of
Church councils and of the papacy itself by sending his
armies into Italy. Pope Paul was forced to take action to
infuse new strength into the Church. He proposed to begin
with the *Curia* itself, for he maintained that no significant
reformation of the Church could be accomplished without
a thorough renovation of its heart and center. He sought

to change the character of personnel by adding new Cardinals as rapidly as possible. In a few cases the appointees were unworthy of their high calling, for they included two of the Pope's nephews. But they also included some of the most distinguished men of the time—for example, Reginald Pole of England, Gasparo Contarini of Venice, Giano Pietro Caraffa, first Superior of the Theatine order, and John du Bellay, Bishop of Paris.

With so successful a transfusion of new blood into the Sacred College, Pope Paul appointed a commission of Cardinals to study the need for reform and to make recommendations. The report of the commission, submitted in 1537, complained of the appointment of unworthy men to Church offices, of the sale of benefices, indulgences and dispensations, and of indolence and neglect of duties by cardinals. In a separate statement Cardinal Bishop Contarini denounced the theory of the absolute authority of the Pope, which he regarded as the source of most of the glaring abuses responsible for the Lutheran revolt. Declaring that "The law of Christ is a law of freedom," he questioned whether that can be called a government "of which the rule is the will of one man, by nature prone to evil, and liable to the influence of caprices and affections innumerable?" [4] Paul III took these admonitions in good humor and decided to convoke a general council to reform the whole Church organization. In this resolve he encountered opposition from many of the Cardinals, who feared that a general reform of the Church might lessen their power and privileges. Equally strong opposition came from some of the secular rulers. The German princes opposed the idea of a council lest it lead to a reunion of Christendom and their own subordination to the Holy Roman Empire. They coveted the property of the Church in their own domains and aspired to achieve their ambitions for total absolutism by combining ecclesiastical power with political autocracy. For a time the Emperor Charles V appeared to favor the proposal for a general council, but

[4] Leopold von Ranke, *History of the Popes: Their Church and State* (London: H. G. Bohn, 1853-56), vol. I, pp. 111-12.

he eventually decided that he needed the support of Lutherans in his wars against the Turks and against Francis I. He
was willing, however, to consider any proposals that might
lead to the establishment of harmonious relations between
Lutherans and Catholics. Accordingly, he requested the
Pope to send Cardinal Contarini, well known for his tact
and diplomacy, to a meeting of the Imperial Diet at Ratisbon in 1541 in the hope that some compromise agreement
between Catholics and Protestants might be achieved.

The Diet at Ratisbon was not guided or controlled by
Contarini. Instead, it was dominated by Charles V, largely
for political purposes. On account of his wars with foreign
states he was anxious to win the support of both his
Lutheran and his Catholic subjects. Contarini showed little
disposition to compromise on what he regarded as the
essentials of Catholic doctrine. He was willing to concede
enough to meet the Lutheran position on the Trinity and
even on justification by faith alone, but he would yield
nothing on transubstantiation and the character of the
sacraments. On these issues, he held, no compromise was
possible. Under the persuasion of Charles, the Diet finally
decided that the principles on which there was general
agreement should be accepted by all citizens of the Empire,
while other issues would be left in abeyance until the meeting of a Church council. Meanwhile, no punishment would
be inflicted upon dissenters. As a result of these decisions,
Charles won the support of his Lutheran subjects in his
wars with the King of France and the Turks. The Catholics
were annoyed, however, that the Emperor should presume
to settle issues of religion. According to the medieval
Catholic view, the Emperor and all other secular rulers
were supposed to assist and protect the Church, and not
attempt to dictate its policies.

Paul III's last days were embittered by family and political troubles growing out of his bestowal of Parma and
Piacenza, states of the Church, upon his illegitimate son
Pier Luigi. In spite of frustrations, Paul III's reform accomplishments were substantial. He abolished the most
flagrant abuses in connection with the sale of dispensations

and other forms of ecclesiastical authority. He recognized
the Society of Jesus and re-established the Roman Inquisition in a commission of Cardinals, soon to be called the
Holy Office. Most important of all, he initiated measures
for convening the Council of Trent, destined to be the
major instrumentality of the Catholic Reformation.

Julius III. As successor to Paul III, the Cardinals
chose Julius III, who reigned for six years. Though before
his election, Julius had committed himself to reform and
the extirpation of heresy, errors in judgment precluded his
making any notable achievements. For one thing, he appointed as a Cardinal a nephew notorious for the sins of
his private life. For another, he antagonized Henry II,
King of France, by refusing to support him in his struggle
with the Emperor. He aroused the displeasure of the Emperor himself by appointing as president of the Council of
Trent a vigorous champion of papal monarchy and the old
theology. Nevertheless, by the time of his death in 1555,
Julius seemed to have set the stage for a Catholic revival
more intense and fanatical than any the Church had yet
seen.

Paul IV. The next and most determined of the reform Popes was Paul IV (1555-1559). Before his election
he was Giovanni Pietro Caraffa, Cardinal-Archbishop of
Naples and one of the principal founders of the Order of
Theatines. Stiff-necked and self-righteous, he regarded his
elevation to the papacy as the work of God. A man of
violent passions and ungovernable hatreds, he aroused the
opposition of powerful rulers and churchmen alike and
foreclosed the return of some wavering Protestants to the
Roman fold. Though seventy-nine years of age when he
mounted St. Peter's throne, he developed ambitions for
enlarging papal authority that surpassed even those of his
youngest predecessors. Early in his reign he devoted much
of his energy to attempts to reduce the political power of
the "accursed Spaniards" in Italy. But the appearance before Rome in 1557 of a powerful army under the Duke of
Alva convinced him that it was the will of God that he
should abandon political activity and give all his attention

to religious reform. Accordingly, he concluded a treaty with the Spaniards and urged that Philip II be considered a pillar of Catholicism.

As a leader of the Catholic Reformation, Paul IV was active not only through the exercise of his own authority as Supreme Pontiff but especially through the agency of the Council of Trent. He dominated this Council as no other leader could be expected to have done.

THE COUNCIL OF TRENT

Convoking the Council. The initial steps for convoking the Council of Trent were taken by Pope Paul III. By 1542 he had gained so much prestige from his reforming activities that he felt strong enough to summon the prelates of Latin Christendom to a great assemblage to consider what further steps might be taken to purify and strengthen the Church. As a meeting place he selected the city of Trent near the Austrian Tyrol. The choice of this city fulfilled the requirement of Charles V that the council meet on territory of the Empire. At the same time, Trent had the advantage of being located on the Italian side of the Alps, a location that would make possible domination of the meetings by the Pope.

Despite the failure of the Conciliar movement a council was still held to be the logical instrument for revitalizing the Church. Recognition of this principle was virtually unanimous except by the Popes themselves and the members of the *Curia*. The former had reason to fear that a council might again declare itself the supreme authority in the Church, as had happened at Constance. Members of the *Curia* worried over the possibility that the reforming zeal of a council might lead to the reduction of their privileges and the abolition of their principal sources of revenue. It is said that the very mention of a council resulted in a sharp decline in the prices of salable Church offices. The pressures, however, were well-nigh irresistible. Leading clerics, both Catholic and Protestant, recognized in a council the only hope of reuniting the international Church. On the political side, no one was more anxious to effect such a union than Charles V and his Imperial supporters. Faced as it was by military threats from the French and the Turks, the Holy Roman Empire could continue to be divided between Lutherans and Catholics only under peril of extinction.

The call for the Council of Trent was issued in the summer of 1542. In the Bull of Convocation, Pope Paul III summoned all bishops, abbots, generals of orders, and representatives of the universities to come to Trent for the opening meeting on November 1. He also invited the Emperor, the King of France, and other secular rulers to participate in the assemblage either in person or through their representatives. For various reasons, chief among which was the outbreak of war between Francis I and Charles V, the Council did not meet until December, 1545. With the advantages of a splendid army and an alliance with the Turks, the King of France was determined to dispose, once and for all, of his old enemy, the Emperor. To the dismay of the latter, the Pope resolved to remain neutral. In the mind of Charles this policy was equivalent to enmity toward him. He denounced Francis as a traitor to Christendom, accused him of prime responsibility for the division of the Church, and questioned the sincerity of the Pope in calling a Church council so long as he refused to take up the challenge thrown down by the French King. As a consequence of these antagonisms both Francis I and Charles V declined to send representatives to the Council of Trent. The result was to leave its initial deliberations overwhelmingly in the hands of the Italians.

Organization of the Council. When the Council finally met in December 1545, plans for its organization and procedure were quite inchoate. The principal delegates present included three Legates, appointed by the Pope to preside over the Council; one Cardinal; four archbishops; twenty-one bishops; and five Generals of Orders. From the beginning the Legates manipulated their functions in such a way as to make the Council an instrument of papal supremacy. They beat down a proposal of the reform party that the title of the Council include a phrase implying its supreme authority. They vetoed an old custom in church councils of voting by nations and substituted voting by individuals. It was obvious under this procedure that the Italians would have a majority. The Legates managed also to confine the voting to bishops and heads of religious orders. Again, this maneuver favored the Italians and also the papacy. Italian bishoprics were small and there were many of them. Furthermore, they depended largely upon the See of Peter for their revenues. Finally, the adoption of a rule that no absent bishop could vote by proxy also favored the Italians. Bishoprics beyond the Alps were commonly large. The incumbents, in many cases, did not dare to leave them lest their territories be swept by heresy or by religious revolution.

The First Assembly. The Council of Trent passed through three stages or Assemblies. The first extended from December 1545 to March 1547. After less than two years of deliberations, the meeting place of the Council was transferred by Paul III to Bologna because of increasingly aggressive attempts by Charles V to influence the delegates. But Charles refused to recognize the legality of the Council of Bologna. As a consequence, it accomplished nothing, and after another two years the Pope suspended it.

Doctrinal Issues. The First Assembly of the Council of Trent concerned itself almost entirely with doctrinal issues, although doctrine and the correction of abuses were supposed to be discussed simultaneously. The delegates included a strong reform faction, under the leadership of Cardinals Contarini, Pole, and Seripando. They believed that the correction of abuses was not only desirable in itself but was the *sine qua non* for reconciliation with the Protestants. They encountered stiff opposition, however, from the Jesuit Cardinal Caraffa, who stood for the stern eradication of all heresies, regardless of any effects such action might have in preventing the reunion of the Church. As events turned out, only three disciplinary reforms received the approval of the delegates. One regulated the teaching of theology, preaching, and the collection of alms. Two others dealt with the residence of bishops and with pluralities, exemptions, and the legal affairs of the clergy. But the

Council refused to classify episcopal residence as a divine
obligation and authorized the Pope to grant dispensations
permitting absenteeism and the holding of more than one
benefice. Abuses, as a consequence, continued, especially
among the higher clergy.

The Bible and Church Tradition. With respect to
doctrinal issues, the Council addressed itself first to the
relative importance of the Scriptures and the traditions of
the Church. The two were declared to be of equal importance as embodiments of divine revelation. As for the
Bible, the Vulgate edition of St. Jerome was agreed to be
the authoritative text. The right to interpret the Scriptures,
however, was declared to rest exclusively in the Church,
which alone had the power of the Holy Ghost. The effect
was to place the judgments of the Church in regard to both
doctrine and practice beyond challenge or question. (*See
Reading No. 6A.*)

Original Sin. The Council turned next to the question of original sin, which raised the complicated issues
of freedom of the will and justification by faith. Protestants,
almost without exception, had adopted the doctrine that
man's nature was totally depraved as a consequence of the
sin of the first parents of the race. Since man's will, therefore, was in bondage, he could perform no meritorious act
by his own efforts. He was constantly prone to fall into
sin and error and could only be saved by the grace of God.
By sincere and abundant faith, though, he could justify
himself before God and make himself worthy of receiving
the divine grace. But no deeds of piety, benevolence, or
charity would facilitate this result. The theologians of the
Council of Trent went back to St. Thomas and revived the
doctrine that human nature was not wholly depraved or
corrupted as a result of Adam's transgression. It was the
consequence of sin, they held, rather than sin itself that
was transmitted to Adam's descendants. Many centuries
after Adam, the coming of the Christ had its effect in mold-
ing the nature of man. The supreme sacrifice on the cross
earned enough merit to redeem all the myriad generations
of men who would live ever after. The Church with its
power to renew this sacrifice through the sacrament of the

Eucharist would impart some of the merit of Christ to the souls of men, and thereby contribute an important element to their eventual salvation.

Justification. The Council decree on justification was one of its most carefully considered pronouncements. It included more than thirty canons or rules condemning the Protestant position. According to the Tridentine statement, justification by faith alone was an impossibility. Faith, the statement said, is not enough. Hope and charity must also be present. In addition, man must have the grace of God to enable him to walk in the paths of righteousness. This grace he receives in the first instance from baptism, but it is augmented by the other sacraments, especially by the Eucharist through which the Church imparts some of the excess merit of the Christ. Man's will is not really in bondage, for he can accept the grace of God or refuse it depending upon his attitude toward the sacraments. By having the sacraments regularly administered for his benefit, he not only accepts divine grace but cooperates with God in achieving his soul's salvation. It was, therefore, the Tridentine position that both faith and good works were essential to complete the process of justification. And since the sacraments, the principal examples of good works, could be administered only by the clergy (with the exception of baptism in emergencies), the result was to give a vigorous boost to the strength of the Church. (*See Readings Nos. 6B and C.*)

The Second Assembly. The Second Assembly of the Council of Trent met in 1551-1552. Convoked by Pope Julius III, it suffered from limitations that did not apply to its predecessor. For one thing, the representation was narrower. No delegates from France attended, since King Henry II was annoyed because the Pope would not support him in his war with the Emperor. Moreover, for a variety of reasons few German or Spanish prelates attended either. Perhaps they feared that papal domination would be stronger than ever, since Julius III had designated as president of the Council Cardinal Crescenzio, an ardent proponent of papal supremacy and the old theology. As a gesture to the German Catholics, who emphasized reconciliation, the Protestants were commanded to send representatives. They came, and presented a statement; but its main effect was simply to show how wide a gulf separated Protestants from Catholics. The conservative Cardinals who dominated the Council were hardly even willing to discuss the proposal of the German delegates that communion in "both kinds" should be permitted, i.e., that the laity as well as the clergy be allowed to partake of both the wine and the bread in the sacrament of the Eucharist. The Council reaffirmed the dogma of transubstantiation, but did little else with respect to either doctrine or practice. After scarcely more than a year and a half its sessions were suspended. The chief cause was the outbreak of a revolt by one of Charles V's former allies, Maurice of Saxony. After a succession of victories, he led his Protestant followers south to the vicinity of Innsbruck and placed both Emperor and Council in a perilous position.

Long Interlude. Following its suspension in 1552, the Council of Trent did not meet for ten years. The explanation lay partly in the fact that many of the old rulers had passed from the scene. King Francis I of France had died in 1547 and his successor, Henry II, twelve years later. The Emperor Charles V had abdicated his various thrones in 1555-1557. Queen Mary of England had died in 1558. Their successors, such monarchs as Philip II of Spain, the Emperor Ferdinand I, and Queen Elizabeth I of England were more keenly interested in the development of their own realms than they were in solving the religious problems of Europe. The new Pope, Paul IV, was preoccupied with zeal for reform and cared little about doctrinal disputes. Moreover, he was obsessed with the necessity of curtailing Spanish influence in Italy and devoted much energy to that. But finding this activity a hindrance to his work of reform, he concluded a treaty with Philip II acclaiming him as a bulwark of the true faith. The ensuing peace impressed most of the other sovereigns as eminently worth preserving, since they had grown weary of strife and uncertainty. Finally, many of the leaders of the Roman clergy had grown pessimistic regarding the possibilities of a Catholic-Protestant reconciliation. They had adopted the view that about all the Church could hope for was to consolidate what it had left and perhaps to recover a small portion of what it had lost—by education, preaching, and persuasion.

The Third Assembly. So unpopular was Paul IV because of his political involvements and his passion for austerity and repression that after his death in 1559 the Cardinals chose as the new Pope a modest man of humble family who disdained political ambitions. He took the name of Pius IV and selected as his assistant the able and distinguished Charles Borromeo, Cardinal of Milan. In November 1560, Pope Pius issued a bull commanding the Council of Trent to reconvene the following Easter. So great was the contention, however, that no session could be held until January 1562. The delegates divided principally into two factions, a curial faction, composed mainly of Italian clergy; and an ultra-montane faction, composed of Spaniards, Imperialists, and French. The Spaniards, with the support of Philip II, demanded a thorough reform of the papacy and a reduction of its powers, but they vigorously opposed any changes in doctrine or ritual. By contrast, the Emperor Ferdinand, with the encouragement of the French and Bavarian prelates, insisted that the Council make doctrinal concessions in the hope of winning back the moderate Protestants and placating the more liberal Catholics. They recommended communion in both kinds, permission for the marriage of priests, celebration of the Mass in the vernacular, reform of the papal *Curia*, limitation of the use of excommunication, and abolition of dispensations.

Dissension among the factions eventually contributed substantially to papal domination of the Third Assembly of the Council. By skillful intrigue and diplomacy Pope Pius IV played the secular rulers off against one another in such a way as to enhance his own supremacy. He encouraged them to look to him for leadership in carrying out reforms rather than to their own representatives in the Council. In a few instances, at least, he resorted to means that were little short of bribery. For example, he won over to his side the Emperor Ferdinand partly by giving his consent to the election of the Emperor's son Maximilian as King of the Romans. He also made clever use of the Jesuits as a body of "shock troops" in rounding up votes, in manipulating debates, and in conducting intrigue at the courts of the principal rulers. By such means he was able to reduce the initial chaos to a semblance of order and to control the Council throughout the Third Assembly.

Despite its unpromising beginning, the Third Assembly of the Council of Trent accomplished more than did either of its predecessors. In the category of reforms were (1) abolition of the office of indulgence seller; (2) provision for the establishment of theological seminaries in every diocese; (3) revision and strengthening of the Index of Prohibited Books originally established by Paul IV; (4) definition of the authority and responsibilities of bishops, particularly with respect to the ordination of priests and supervision of their conduct.

The achievements with respect to doctrine were, if not more numerous, at least more significant. The Council reaffirmed nearly all of the doctrines challenged by the Protestants. Included were: the belief in purgatory, the invocation of saints, the apostolic succession of the priesthood, celibacy for all grades of the clergy, the supremacy of the Pope over every bishop and priest, the definition of the Mass as a renewal of Christ's sacrifice on the cross, the validity of communion in one kind for the laity ("Christ is whole and entire under either species."), and the approval of indulgences, provided they were not granted for monetary payment. (*See Readings Nos. 6B and C.*)

Close of the Council. The Third Assembly of the Council of Trent came to an almost abrupt end in 1563. By that time the various factions had grown weary of it. Moreover, they feared that attempts to settle the remaining issues would provoke angry controversy and would antagonize some of the secular princes. Important also was the realization that the Council had become a rubber stamp for the papacy. As early as 1562, Pope Pius IV had made what appeared to be a wanton display of his power. He had appointed as Cardinals two boys, eighteen and eleven years of age, respectively. He had elevated as bishops persons under age and without degrees. And he had loaded dioceses with ruinous financial burdens in order to provide incomes for his favorites. His Legates at the Council capped the climax by frankly proclaiming that their sole objective was to strengthen the papal authority as rapidly as possible and then to dissolve the Council. As a result of these developments, the Assembly was in an uproar. In March the Emperor Ferdinand sent a letter to the Pope denouncing him for delaying reform of the Church and enslaving the Council. But Pius IV knew full well the weaknesses of the opposition. Its forces were divided, and its chief, the Emperor, was a feeble and irresolute leader. The Pope proceeded to appoint as his chief Legate, the shrewd and skillful Cardinal Morone and charged him with the mission of weaning the Emperor away from the opposition. Morone succeeded, as did Cardinal Lorraine in softening the heart of the King of France. In March 1563, both rulers gave their consent to the closing of the Council. During the succeeding nine months all went well for the cause of papal supremacy, and in December 1563, Cardinal Morone, as chief presiding officer, declared the Council closed.

The Council of Trent was the last ecumenical council of the Roman Church before the Vatican Council of 1869-1870. But the Council of Trent was hardly universal in any proper sense of the term. The Italian delegates numbered two-thirds of the total. Spain sent about thirty, France about twenty, and Germany no more than eight. Nor did the Tridentine Council enjoy the independence possessed by some of its predecessors. The whole course of its action was governed by the presupposition that it had no autonomous status, and that its functions were to be discharged completely under the agency and guidance of the Pope. The papal Legates, as presiding officers, confined the discussion to subjects submitted by the Pope, and they seem frequently to have taken the position that he was not bound by the vote of the majority. In some cases the decision of difficult issues was left entirely to him. And at the close of the sessions a resolution was adopted according to which enactments of the Council on moral reform and ecclesiastical discipline were subject to the condition that they must not operate to the prejudice of papal authority.

Significance of the Council.   Despite its limitations, the Council of Trent was undoubtedly one of the most significant events in the history of the Church. It marked a kind of climax of the crusading zeal for reform from within that had had its origin in the closing years of the fifteenth century. It was also the first major defensive effort of the Church against the inroads of Protestantism. But in a sense the Tridentine movement was a reaction against the liberal tendencies manifesting themselves among some of the clergy. The spirit of Trent was autocracy, repression, and domination. Though the Council's reform achievements were commendable, some of the most glaring abuses such as the *annates* and the superstitious veneration of relics were not even touched. Praise can be accorded to the successful attempts at clearer definition of doctrine, but it would be hard to find justification for the assertions of papal supremacy that amounted almost to an endorsement of absolutism. This presupposition was a defiance of the whole trend toward ecclesiastical democracy that had characterized the Conciliar movement. The Council of Trent did not clearly assert the infallibility of the Pope, but by abdicating so many of its functions to him or his Legates, it prepared the way for a definite assertion of that dogma by the Vatican Council of 1870. So far as reconciliation with the Protestants was concerned, the Council of Trent was a failure. By its views on justification by faith and the equal validity of the Scriptures and Church tradition, the Council made such a reconciliation impossible. Justification by faith alone was a fundamental article in the creed of nearly all Protestants, and so was the belief in the exclusive divine authority of the Scriptures.

There were other manifestations also of a spirit of intolerance and unreason emanating from the Tridentine Council. One was the establishment of the Index of Prohibited Books. Another was the revival of the Inquisition, or Holy Office. Founded in the Middle Ages for the extirpation of such heresies as Albigensianism and used extensively in Spain against the Moors and Jews, the Inquisition was reconstituted at Rome during the pontificate of Paul IV. As in former times it proved a convenient agency for harnessing the punitive powers of the state to the Church and thereby making possible the execution of sentences of burning or beheading without involving the clergy directly in the shedding of blood.

Despite pretensions of returning to the philosophy of St. Thomas Aquinas, the Council of Trent seemed anxious to establish the supremacy of faith over reason instead of bringing the two into harmony. Its Catechism included the following admonition: "When God commands us to believe, he does not propose to have us search into his divine judgments, nor to inquire their reasons and causes, but demands an immutable faith . . . Faith, therefore, excludes not only all doubt, but even the desire of subjecting its truth to demonstration." It appeared to be a basic premise of St. Thomas that no real conflict existed between reason and faith. Virtually the whole Christian theology could be reduced to a rational explanation. Only a few of the most recondite doctrines, such as the doctrine of the Incarnation, needed to be taken entirely on faith. Subjecting the truths of the Christian religion to "demonstration" was the thing he considered most essential.

— 6 —

THE CATHOLIC REFORMATION
AFTER TRENT

The Council of Trent a Turning Point. It is tempting
to regard the Council of Trent as the culmination of the
great Catholic reform movement of the sixteenth century.
It is more accurate to think of it as a turning point in
that movement. In the early sixteenth century the Church
was still a hotbed of intrigue and scheming for political
and economic advantages. Cardinals and bishops were
more concerned with threats to their revenues and privileges
than they were with the obligations of religion. Popes, in
many cases, were elevated to their high position as a result
of maneuvering by powerful families, such as the Medici
and the Borgias. In a number of instances they were men
who, before their election, had led scandalous lives. The
Church itself, and particularly its center in Rome, had
most of the characteristics of a secular state. It waged war,
coined money, entered into alliances, employed mercenary
troops, conquered territory, and constantly strove for
larger revenues to support a luxurious court. Though intrigue did not entirely disappear from the election of Popes
after the Council of Trent, most of the Cardinals now
appeared sincerely desirous of choosing well-qualified can-
didates. At any rate, the Popes during the latter part of the
century were generally superior to their predecessors. They
devoted themselves with earnestness and conviction to
applying and enforcing the reforms of the Tridentine code.
It must be admitted, however, that they had the advantage
of a more stable political environment. Italy was no longer
torn by internal wars, and the Church was not harassed or

in danger of its very existence. Instead, it was able to take the offensive in Poland and in the southern and eastern provinces of the Empire and thereby to check the advancing tide of Protestantism.

The Post-Trentine Popes: Pius V. Much of the credit for Catholic reform after Trent must be given to the succession of superior Popes that began with the election of Pius V in 1566. The new Pope was a paragon of virtue and austerity. Of humble origin, he rose to be prior of a Dominican convent, bishop, Cardinal, and Grand Inquisitor by sheer reputation for indefatigable work and blameless conduct. His election as Pontiff was also in recognition of his probity and was supposed to have been quite unexpected. As Pope he continued the same austere and dedicated life he had led as a friar. He ate and drank very little, prayed until the tears came, and spent entire weeks in meditation or on exhausting pilgrimages. He proclaimed stringent regulations against Sabbath-breaking, simony, blasphemy, and concubinage. He ordered that adulterers of both sexes be punished by public whipping, imprisonment, or exile. In accordance with the Tridentine code, he required that the children of Rome be sent to Church on Sunday afternoons to learn Christian doctrine. He was especially interested in the moral improvement of both secular and regular clergy. He forbade the Cardinals to eat from silver plate and tried to recall the members of religious orders to observance of their vow of poverty. Finally, he encouraged the founding of new orders to set examples of devotion and service to all who wished to take their religion seriously. Among them were the Carmelite order, the Brothers of Mercy (for the service of patients in hospitals), and a severer branch of Observants or orthodox Franciscans.

Gregory XIII. The activities of the next Pope, Gregory XIII (1572-1585), provided an interesting complement to the work of Pius V. Gregory had been a successful professor of law at the University of Bologna, and had held legal, administrative, and diplomatic posts under Popes Paul III and Paul IV. Though he was not so renowned an ascetic as Pius V, he did not turn back the clock to the scandalous practices of former days. He was an indefatigable worker and devout worshiper, and he evidently expected the same qualities in his subordinates. He refused to sanction the appointment of bishops by secular rulers unless the persons selected were fully qualified. In contrast with some of his pre-Trentine predecessors, he gave no official favors to his nephews or to the sons he had begotten before his priesthood. He was concerned primarily with reforms of an administrative or organizational character. To facilitate these he created new congregations of Cardinals, for the revision of canon law, for reform of the ceremonial, and for the preparation of a new edition of the Scriptures. For more rigorous enforcement of the decrees of Trent, he appointed a special committee of four Cardinals comprising the most rigid reformers in the Church. In order that priests might be better educated and more strongly fortified for their moral responsibilities he founded numerous colleges in Rome and entrusted their conduct to the Society of Jesus. The central one of these became the Gregorian University and attracted some of the most illustrious scholars of Europe.

Sixtus V. The reign of the next Pope, Sixtus V (1585-1590), constituted in a measure a setback in the progress toward a better Church. A child of extreme poverty, Sixtus seems never to have acquired the urbanity and restraint so necessary for success in the large undertakings of high office. He conceived violent dislikes for his superiors and pursued his own ambitions with reckless disregard for some of the consequences. He undoubtedly possessed many abilities, but his advancement came largely as a result of favors bestowed by influential clerics. As head of the Church he had the consuming ambition to make the papacy independent and powerful. Pursuit of this ambition led him to revive corrupt practices that had been well on the road to eradication by his predecessors. He revived the sale of papal offices, setting specified prices for the various grades. He also sold knighthoods in lavish profusion. He inflicted burdensome taxation upon the inhabitants of the States of the Church. By such means he accumulated a massive hoard in which he took great pride. Some of it he expended on public works, but the bulk of it he set aside for grandiose political projects. He dreamed of annihilating the Turks, conquering Egypt, transporting the Holy Sepulchre to Italy, and placing his nephew on the throne of France. Needless to say, conditions in Europe did not foster the realization of any of these fantasies.

Yet on the constructive side the record of Sixtus V was not unimpressive. He reorganized the College of Cardinals, fixing the number of its members at seventy. He awarded red hats only to men of virtue and integrity. He enforced the requirement of diocesan residence upon bishops and even upon Cardinals. He insisted that bishops pay regular visits to Rome, at intervals ranging from three to ten years depending upon the distance involved. Though he created new courts of the Inquisition, he dealt rather leniently with accused persons. He was more rigorous in punishing ordinary criminals. By hunting down thousands of brigands he made the States of the Church tranquil and safe. Despite his lack of scholarly aptitude, he worked on a revision of the Index and a new edition of the Vulgate. But he never finished the former, and he took no steps to proclaim the latter the official version of the Church. Though he died execrated by his own subjects, he deserved a better reputation than he has generally been given.

The Later Popes. The three Popes who immediately succeeded Sixtus V contributed almost nothing to the Catholic Reformation. The chief reason, perhaps, was the brevity of their pontificates. Urban VII reigned for only ten days, Gregory XIV for ten months, and Innocent IX for fourteen months. Reform activity was not resumed until the pontificate of Clement VIII (1592-1605). He and his four successors, Paul V, Gregory XV, Urban VIII, and Innocent X continued papal policy along the lines developed by Pius V and Gregory XIII. They simplified further and made more efficient the administrative machinery of the Church. They appointed men distinguished for learning as well as for virtue to the chief offices and thereby raised the hierarchy to a position of respect. They founded new orders and compelled older ones to observe their rules and discipline more strictly. They canonized a number of the great leaders of the Reformation period, including Charles Borromeo, Ignatius of Loyola, Francis Xavier, and Gaetano di Tiene. The Catholic Reformation may be considered to have reached its final climax during the pontificate of Innocent X (1644-1655). During the Jubilee of 1650 Pope Innocent prayed with the crowd in every ceremony and infused a new piety and sense of solidarity into the minds and hearts of all Catholics.

Post-Trentine Activities of the Jesuits. It would be a mistake, of course, to assume that all of the work of the post-Trentine Reformation was done by the Popes. Much of it can be credited to the Jesuits, whose activities have already been covered in Chapter 3. True, the Jesuits were not so much interested in reform as they were in combating heterodoxy and strengthening the position of the Church. But they soon found that it was impossible to achieve the latter without eradicating at least the most grievous of the abuses that had weakened the Church in the first place. Moreover, some of them reached the conclusion that God would automatically reward an amendment of morals by a miraculous correction of unorthodox doctrine.

But for the most part the Jesuits relied upon education and evangelization. They procured the appointment of *nuncios* to the various courts of northern and central Europe. They sent their preachers into Bavaria, Austria, Switzerland, Bohemia, and Poland to persuade the inhabitants of the need to return to the ancient faith. They established colleges at Würzburg, Augsburg, Coblenz, Erfurt, and Trier in Germany and at Braunsberg, Jaroslav, Wilna, and Lublin in Poland. Their colleges and academies were founded mostly for the instruction of upper-class youths, since Jesuit leaders like Peter Canisius believed that persons of all conditions would be drawn toward the example set by "the great." Nevertheless, provision was made in some of the schools for the education of poor students free of charge. Canisius himself arranged for the admission of 200 of these at Augsburg as early as 1560. The result of the preaching and teaching of the Jesuits was a religious revival of truly heroic proportions in some parts of central Europe. Poland, for example, was recovered for the Catholic faith. In Switzerland such crowds of worshipers thronged the churches that there were not enough priests to administer the sacraments. In 1575 only 300 communicants attended the parish churches of Lucerne. By 1589 the number is said to have risen to more than 12,000.[5] Men were reported to have given up drinking, dancing, and gambling; and public women to have left the streets and taken vows of chastity.

The Inquisition.   Much credit, if such it can be called, must also be given to the Inquisition. Founded in the Middle Ages for the extirpation of such heresies as Albigensianism, the Inquisition was established in Spain by Ferdinand and Isabella as an instrument of their crusade against the Moors and the Jews. It was also used later, with unexampled fury, against Protestants. In 1542 a Roman Inquisition was established or reconstituted. Pope Paul III appointed six high-ranking clerics as Inquisitors-General with jurisdiction "throughout Christendom including Italy and the Roman Curia." They were to investigate all and single out those who "wandered from the way of the Lord and the Catholic faith, as well as those suspected of heresy." The "guilty and the suspects" were to be imprisoned and proceeded against "up to the final sentence." The Pope seemed to take it for granted that in most cases the final sentence would be capital punishment, for after the death of the accused his goods might be "put up for sale." The procedure of the Inquisition at Rome, according to Cardinal Seripando, was at first less terrifying than that of its Spanish counterpart. He admitted that later, however, the Roman Inquisition "acquired such a reputation that from no other judgment-seat on earth were more horrible and fearful sentences to be expected." [6]

The Inquisition was undoubtedly one of the most effective weapons of the Church in maintaining its power in such countries as Italy and Spain. Although coercion and threats of coercion are seldom successful in stamping out

[5] Pierre Janelle, *The Catholic Reformation* (Milwaukee: The Bruce Publishing Co., 1949), pp. 273-74.

[6] Quoted by Preserved Smith, *The Age of the Reformation* (New York: Henry Holt and Co., 1920), p. 417.

ideas, they can be readily effective in enforcing conformity to established rules and practices. Thus a Christian might firmly believe in justification by faith alone, and even his most intimate friends might not be aware of it; but failure to partake of the sacraments would immediately raise suspicion and would probably result in punishment. The procedure of the Inquisition was well calculated to make it a terrifying instrument of repression. All trials were secret. The accused was presumed guilty even though he had been arrested on mere suspicion. Both witnesses and accused persons were subject to torture. The early Church had opposed torture, but in 1252 Innocent IV approved its use for the discovery of heresy. Nevertheless, all confessions were considered "voluntary." Procedure in the courts of the Inquisition involved no litigation. The judges were also the prosecutors, and no lawyer could defend the accused without incurring himself the guilt of heresy. According to H. C. Lea, "there was never any case of formal acquittal, even though guilt was not proved." [7] Convicted heretics were given an opportunity to confess and repent. Those who did so were condemned to perpetual imprisonment. Obstinate heretics who refused to confess and abjure their crimes were turned over to the secular arm. In effect, this was equivalent to a sentence of death, usually by burning, though sometimes the burning was preceded by strangling.

The courts of the Inquisition did not confine their jurisdiction to trials of accused heretics. They also prosecuted and condemned persons on charges of blasphemy, sorcery, sodomy, and usury. Even the dead were sometimes tried for crimes committed during their lifetime. If convicted, punishment might be inflicted upon their descendants. Legacies might be confiscated, and the children and grandchildren prohibited from holding office. Of course, the severity of penalties varied from one country to another. They were undoubtedly most severe in Spain. About 2,000 persons were burned during the eighteen years that the Spanish Inquisition was under the command of the infamous Torquemada. On the other hand, the use of torture

[7] *A History of the Inquisition of the Middle Ages* (New York: Harper and Brothers, 1887), vol. I, p. 453.

was originally opposed by the Spaniards. Alphonso X of Aragon (1252-1284) prohibited it. It was revived, however, after the consolidation of the Spanish kingdom, and applied shamelessly in the sixteenth and seventeenth centuries. It was not abolished in all tribunals of the Inquisition until 1816.

The Index. Included as one of the repressive agencies of the Inquisition was the Index of Prohibited Books. Censorship and destruction of heretical writings were among the oldest examples of ecclesiastical tyranny. The Apostle Paul persuaded the Ephesian sorcerers to burn their books. The early Christian emperors, Theodosius II and Valentinian III, burned the writings of the Nestorians and the Manicheans. Justinian destroyed the Talmud. In the thirteenth century Pope Alexander IV ordered the burning of the writings of William of St. Amour, Rector of the University of Paris, because of his attacks upon the Dominicans and Franciscans. But censorship on an extensive scale did not begin until after the invention of printing. Fear that important books of the Church might gain wide circulation and fall into the hands of ignorant people incapable of interpreting them correctly led some of the Popes to institute measures of control. In 1501 Alexander VI issued a decree forbidding the printing of any book in any diocese without the approval of the local bishop.

The plan for a complete catalogue of forbidden books emanated from secular rather than from ecclesiastical sources. In 1546 the University of Louvain, at the instigation of the Emperor, drew up an extensive list and enlarged it four years later. It contained a number of unauthorized editions of the Bible, together with the works of such unorthodox theologians as Luther, Calvin, Oecolampadius, Melanchthon, Hus, and Zwingli. Curiously, the writings of Erasmus were not included. The issuance of the Louvain catalogue influenced the Roman Inquisition to publish its own list. In 1557 it issued a decree commanding the public burning of the works of Machiavelli, Poggio, and Erasmus. A much more complete list was issued two years later by Pope Paul IV. Officially designated the Index of Prohibited Books, it divided questionable writings into three classes: (1) writings composed by men whose general philosophy was in error and all of whose books were therefore condemned; (2) writings whose authors had erred only occasionally and whose works were therefore not all condemned; and (3) anonymous writings.

In 1562 the Council of Trent turned its attention to the issue of forbidden books. It adopted a resolution providing that inasmuch as heresy had not been eliminated by repression, the censorship should be made stricter. For this purpose a commission was appointed comprising four archbishops, nine bishops, two generals of orders, and some lesser officials. The results of the work of this commission were published by Pope Paul IV under the name of the Tridentine Index. The categories adopted by the commission for placing books on the forbidden list included the following: (1) books published before 1515 and condemned by Popes or councils; (2) unauthorized versions of the Bible; (3) heretical books; (4) obscene books; and (5) books on witchcraft and necromancy.

In order to keep the Index up to date, it was obvious that successive revisions would be necessary. To provide for these, Pope Pius V appointed a special Congregation of the Index, which has survived into modern times. More than forty separate Indices have thus far been issued. In addition to keeping the Index up to date, the Congregation also has the function of expurgating books. From time to time it publishes a separate *Index expurgatorius* indicating the portions of particular books that must be deleted or revised in order to make them acceptable for Catholics.

7

THE COUNTER REFORMATION
AS A POLITICAL MOVEMENT

Soon after the middle of the sixteenth century the Catholic Reformation entered a more distinctly political phase. The change may be accurately described as one of degree rather than of kind. Almost from the beginning the Catholic reform movement had had its political involvements. The Popes ruled over the States of the Church as political despots, and several of them tried to strengthen and expand these States as bastions of ecclesiastical power. Moreover, some of the early reform Popes were intently preoccupied with eliminating Spanish political influence in Italy, despite the fact that the Spaniards had been the real pioneers of the Catholic Reformation. But during the first half of the sixteenth century, regeneration of the Roman Church was not a major concern of the secular rulers of Europe. The kings of France were pursuing a policy of *Realpolitik* which led them successively to invade Italy and to form alliances with Turkey for the aggrandizement of their own power. In order to advance his marital ambitions Henry VIII established a national Church of England under his own headship. During the brief reign of his son, Edward VI, this church became definitely Protestant. The Holy Roman Emperor Charles V, who was also Charles I, King of Spain, had the most complicated problems of all. (*See Reading No. 7C.*) A devout Catholic, he desired to see the Church purified and strengthened. But he had so many Lutherans among his subjects that he could not support the papal policy of eradicating all forms of heresy. Besides, his conception of the Empire as an equal partner with the

Church in guiding the destinies of Christendom made him
suspicious of any activity that might enlarge papal authority.

The New Rulers of Europe.   In 1555-1556 Charles V,
harassed by defeats and frustrations, decided to abdicate
his various thrones. (*See Reading No. 7D.*) That of the
Holy Roman Empire he gave to his brother, Ferdinand I,
who was already King of Bohemia. As Emperor, Ferdinand
obtained for his Protestant subjects a few concessions from
the Pope (mainly the privilege of communion in both kinds
for laymen in Bohemia and some parts of Germany), but
he gave zealous support to the Jesuits, and he upheld the
basic principle of the Treaty of Augsburg: *Cuius regio eius
religio.* (*See Reading No. 7A.*) In accordance with this
principle some of the rulers of petty states within the Empire imposed the Catholic faith upon all their subjects. For
example, Duke Albert V of Bavaria, with the support of
the Pope and the Jesuits, proceeded to stamp out Protestantism in all parts of his domain. Protestant preachers and
teachers were exiled, public officials were required to take
an oath to uphold the decrees of the Council of Trent, a
strict censorship of books was established, and the school
system was reorganized under the control of the Jesuits.

Philip II.   But the most momentous result, so far as
the Catholic Reformation was concerned, of the division
of the Holy Roman Empire by Charles V was the accession
of his son Philip II to the thrones of Spain and the Netherlands. Narrow in outlook, bigoted, and unimaginative,
Philip had almost none of the qualifications that the times
demanded for so important a position. At the middle of the
sixteenth century Spain had a good chance of becoming
the leading nation of Europe. The wealth of her empire
was prodigious. Her control of the Low Countries put her
into a position to dictate to Britain and France. Her king
was also King of Naples and Sicily and Duke of Milan. By
one means or another he controlled Florence, Mantua,
Ferrara, Savoy, Urbino, and the States of the Church. Yet
his ignorance and the narrowness of his policies caused
him to fritter away this rich inheritance. He wasted the
gold and silver that flowed in from the colonies on schemes

to impose dominion by force on most of Europe. He forbade the export of iron, cloth, and leather goods to the colonies in order to increase the supply of such commodities for the home market. He imposed a ten per cent sales tax on all his subjects. Needless to say, his political policies were no less arbitrary and high-handed. He insisted upon directing and regulating every governmental activity. Though he had thirteen consultative councils, he permitted them to initiate nothing. He originated everything, passed upon everything, and controlled everything. Few monarchs have worked harder for what they considered the welfare of their subjects, and few have been more unsuccessful.

Philip was nothing if not a zealous Catholic. He worked with unflagging ardor to make the interests of Spain and the interests of Catholicism identical. Soon after his accession to power he announced a vigorous policy of exterminating heretics. He appeared at a great *auto da fé* in Valladolid where twelve victims condemned by the Inquisition were to be burned to death. As they filed past the king, one of them raised the question why he should be forced to suffer so horrible a punishment. Philip replied: "Had I a son so obstinate as you I would eagerly carry fagots to burn him." Like his predecessors, Philip made extensive use of the Inquisition as an instrument of religious repression. Not even the most pious of his subjects was immune from its investigatory tyranny. Ignatius of Loyola was haled before it for questioning, and St. Teresa was held for two years under arrest at Toledo. Philip also continued with increasing fury the war begun by Ferdinand and Isabella against the Moors. He devoted his efforts especially to the extirpation of the Moriscos, or converted Moors, living in Granada. In 1570 he unleashed a frightful crusade against them which resulted in the sacking of hundreds of their towns and villages and the massacre of their inhabitants. Those who survived were redistributed among the Christian peoples of Castile and Leon.

Philip's record of savage repression in the Netherlands was equally deplorable. By 1565 discontent among the Protestants of the cities and towns of the north became so strong that it flared into open revolt. Religious causes

were, of course, not the only ones. Nationalism was a leading factor also, since Philip persisted in treating the Netherlands as subject provinces. In addition, there were serious
economic grievances—high taxation and the restriction of
commerce for the benefit of Spanish merchants. Nevertheless, it was religious feeling that was largely responsible
for the ferocity of the struggle. Philip II regarded all
Protestants as traitors, and he was determined to root them
out of every territory under his rule. In 1567 he sent the
Duke of Alva with 10,000 soldiers to quell the revolt in
the Netherlands. For six years Alva terrorized the land,
putting hundreds of the rebels to death and torturing or
imprisoning thousands of others. The Protestants retaliated
with almost equal savagery, and the war continued its bar-
barous course until 1609. Its principal result was the establishment of an independent Dutch Republic comprising
the territories now included in the Netherlands. The southern or Belgian provinces, where the majority of the inhabitants were Catholics, returned to Spanish rule.

Queen Mary of England.   Efforts of the government
of England to promote the Counter Reformation were limited almost entirely to the brief reign of Queen Mary
(1553-1558). As we have noted, her father, Henry VIII
(1509-1547), established a national Catholic Church independent of the See of Rome. Under her half-brother,
Edward VI (1547-1553), this church became Protestant.
It was almost inevitable that Mary, when she came to the
throne, should attempt to restore Catholicism. Not only
was she a pious Catholic, but she was convinced that the
majority of her countrymen were not ready to abandon the
faith of their fathers. Moreover, as the daughter of Henry
VIII and Catherine she was bound to associate the begin-
nings of the revolt against Rome with her mother's suffer-
ings. Accordingly, she restored the celebration of the Mass
and the rule of clerical celibacy; and she persuaded Parliament to vote the unconditional return of England to
papal allegiance. But her efforts to restore and strengthen
the Catholic Church in England ended in failure. The
English people were not ready for a Lutheran or Calvinist
revolution, but they were even less in a mood to accept

immediate subjection to Rome. Further, Mary doomed her cause by her marriage to Philip, the ambitious heir to the Spanish throne. Her subjects feared that this union might lead to foreign complications, if not actual domination by Spain. Queen Mary was succeeded in 1558 by her half-sister, Elizabeth I, the redoubtable daughter of Henry VIII and Anne Boleyn. The fate of the Church of England was left to be settled by considerations of practical politics.

The Struggle in France. At first thought it might seem that France would be the nation least inclined to promote or assist the Catholic Reformation. Through the Pragmatic Sanction of Bourges the French kings had obtained virtual independence of Rome. They had abolished the Pope's right to raise revenues and to make appointments in France. They had granted to civil magistrates the power to regulate religious affairs within their own districts. Moreover, the French monarchs surpassed the majority of the sovereigns of Europe in asserting claims to despotic authority. Their methods were Machiavellian, and ideology seemed to make little difference in their decision making at home or in their choice of allies for foreign ventures. But these conditions were variables rather than constants. The death of King Henry II in 1559 ushered in a struggle between rival factions which kept the country in turmoil for upwards of forty years. Henry was succeeded by his son, Francis II, whose wife was the daughter of Duke Claude of Guise. The Guises were ambitious, aggressive, and above all orthodox. The rival faction of Bourbons had its chief center in Navarre, a small principality in southern France. Some of the Bourbons and some of the wealthy nobles and merchants who supported them were Protestants, or Huguenots as they had come to be called. Their ambitions were quite as much political as they were religious, for they considered themselves the rightful claimants to the throne of France.

The pretensions of the Bourbons were deeply resented by the Guises who threatened to harry them out of the land. Under the pretext of suppressing heresy, they inaugurated a severe persecution of the Huguenots. Civil war was the inevitable result. In 1572 the regent, Catherine de

Médici, in the hope of putting an end to the strife, plotted with the Guises to murder the Protestant chiefs. The conspiracy unloosed the ugly passions of the Paris mob, with the result that in less than twenty-four hours (St. Bartholomew's Day) 2,000 Huguenots were slain. The war dragged on until 1593 when Henry of Navarre decided that "Paris was worth a mass" and ascended the throne as His Catholic Majesty Henry IV. The religious issue did not approach a settlement until 1598 when Henry issued the Edict of Nantes granting freedom of conscience to both his Catholic and Huguenot subjects. (*See Reading No. 7B.*) Even this proved only a temporary solution, for the Edict was revoked by Louis XIV in 1685.

8

RESULTS OF THE
COUNTER REFORMATION

Without doubt, the Reformation was one of the most influential movements in the history of the world. It was comparable in scope and significance to the great French Revolution of 1789-1799 or to the Industrial Revolutions starting about 1750. More than any other factor of its time it shaped the transition from the medieval to the modern world. It fostered nationalism, presided over the birth of the modern state system, and gave sanction to the growth of individualism and to the kind of business society that has come to symbolize the capitalist system. True, most of these results are to be associated primarily with the Protestant phase of the Reformation movement. Yet, with respect to some of them, the Catholic Reformation exerted a similar influence. The zeal of Protestants in combating the rationalism and tolerance that sometimes characterized late medieval society was matched by that of Reformation Catholics. Protestant and Catholic reformers held duplicating viewpoints regarding absolutism in church and state. Both gave their support to despotic rule in countries where they constituted a majority of the population. Conversely, they both opposed absolute rule and taught the right of rebellion in countries where they formed but a minority of the total inhabitants. Catholic leaders seemed as anxious as Lutherans to accept the Peace of Augsburg, which gave the prince in each German territory the right to determine whether Catholicism or Lutheranism should be the religion of his subjects. Finally, both Catholics and Protestants accepted the Treaty of Westphalia, which recognized the sovereign equality of all the states of Europe. In so doing they destroyed what was left of medieval universalism and laid the foundations for the modern system of fiercely competing states.

Intolerance.   In turning to the specific results of the Counter Reformation, we may appropriately consider first the religious. One of these was intolerance. The Church had always maintained an elaborate dogmatic system. Without doing so, it probably could not have survived. Yet at times the medieval Church showed an amazing degree of tolerance in permitting deviations from, or even attacks upon, these dogmas. For example, Latin Averroism was tolerated for a considerable time at the University of Paris. The Latin Averroists taught that a doctrine could be false in religion and true in philosophy, or *vice versa*. The tempestuous Abelard seems not to have been called to account for his skeptical and critical teachings. Nor does the record show that Thomas Aquinas was ever rebuked for adopting Aristotle as a fountain of philosophic wisdom instead of relying exclusively upon the Christian Fathers.

Of course, there were examples of tendencies quite the opposite. (*See Reading No. 8A.*) Persecutions for witchcraft were not unknown. (*See Reading No. 8B.*) A full thirty years before the outbreak of the Protestant Revolution, Pope Innocent VIII issued a bull authorizing two agents to proceed against witches in Germany and to punish them, if necessary, by calling on the help of the secular arm. Crusades against heretics were also instigated in the later Middle Ages. The most infamous example was the war for the extermination of the Albigenses launched in the thirteenth century by Count Raymond of Toulouse, with the blessing of Pope Innocent III. In this instance the motives were largely political and economic, but such were not the exclusive factors inciting persecution. The Church had long maintained its right to enforce belief and to punish men for heresy. St. Augustine held that the Church should "compel" non-Christians to come into the fold. St. Thomas Aquinas argued that faith is a virtue and that heretics deserved "not only to be excommunicated but to be put to death."

The Reformation, however, made bigotry and fanaticism almost the normal attitudes and procedures. Luther defended prosecutions and punishments for heresy on the ground that it was necessary to eradicate "blasphemy," but he defined blasphemy so broadly as to include almost any un-Lutheran opinion. His co-worker, Philip Melanchthon, was more explicit when he declared that the denial of original sin, the rejection of infant baptism, and refusal to believe that the elements in the Eucharistic sacrament contained the real body and blood of the Savior were examples of blasphemy properly punishable by death. He demanded to know why good Christians should pity heretics more than does God, who sends all of them without recourse to the flames of Hell. How he could be sure of the accuracy of this statement he did not make clear; nor did he leave any opening for the possibility that what was heresy for one sect might well be orthodoxy for another. John Calvin taught that the death decreed by God in the Old Testament to idolaters was a universal law which all Christians were obligated to impose upon those who rejected the true religion. Those who rejected the death penalty for heretics he classified as heretics themselves who deserved the same penalty.

The Catholic reformers' penchant for bigotry and intolerance was not less conspicuous. The Church condemned not only Luther's radical attacks upon Catholic doctrine but also the more liberal pronouncements of his earlier career. One of these was his assertion that it is against the will of the Holy Ghost to put heretics to death. He thought it sufficient that they should be exiled. The Council of Trent anathematized those who denied the inheritance of original sin, rejected infant baptism, repudiated the necessity of good works as well as faith, argued that man's will is in bondage, held that laymen as well as priests should receive communion in both kinds, and insisted upon the right of priests to marry. Nor was the Council any more tolerant of a dependence upon reason or of critical or inquiring attitudes. One of its decrees said that when God commands us to believe, He demands an "immutable faith." Faith, therefore, would exclude not only all doubt, but even the desire to inquire into the rationality of doctrine. The difference between this judgment and Luther's blast against reason as "the devil's harlot" was mainly one of greater restraint and dignity of language.

When it came to the *practice* of intolerance, Catholic and Protestant reformers followed parallel courses. Indeed, they sometimes joined forces, particularly with respect to the persecution of Anabaptists. It was an alliance of Catholics and Lutherans at the Diet of Spires that passed the decree condemning all Anabaptists to death. Catholic and Protestant actions against individual heretics were also similar. Although the Protestants had no Inquisition operating throughout their territories, they did set up special tribunals in some areas for the trial and punishment of heretics, or they authorized secular governments to exercise these functions directly. Calvin, in the preface to his *Institutes*, argued the right of any government to put heretics to death, contending, of course, that Protestants were not heretics. In pursuance of this principle he approved the burning of Michael Servetus by the government of Geneva for rejecting the doctrine of the Trinity and for teaching that Palestine is a barren country in defiance of the Old Testament description of it as a land flowing with milk and honey.

The most notable instances of persecution of individuals by the Catholic Reformation were those of Galileo Galilei and Giordano Bruno. Galileo was one of the chief founders of modern astronomy. With the aid of the telescope, which he had perfected to a magnifying power of thirty-two times, he discovered the satellites of Jupiter, the rings of Saturn, and spots on the sun. He formulated also the laws of motion and anticipated many of the components of a universal theory of gravitation. It is not an exaggeration to say that these discoveries and demonstrations provided the needed practical foundation for the Copernican hypothesis. And, of course, it was Galileo's conviction of the essential truth of that hypothesis which brought him into conflict with the Church. Galileo seems to have adopted the Copernican theory early in his life but did not avow his opinions until after the beginning of the seventeenth century. In 1616 he was summoned from Florence to Rome by Cardinal Robert Bellarmine, the most powerful member of the Sacred College, and warned to desist from the expression of Copernican views. The consulting theologians of the Inquisition condemned his two propositions that the sun is immovable at the center of the universe, and that the earth has a diurnal rotation, as "contrary to Holy Scripture" and incompatible with the Catholic faith. A short time later Pope Paul V officially admonished him to refrain thenceforth from "holding, teaching, or defending" the condemned doctrines. This admonition Galileo promised to obey. During the next few years, however, conditions at the pontifical court appeared to change. In 1623 Galileo's warmest friend and strongest admirer in the College of Cardinals became Pope as Urban VIII. Galileo was deceived by what seemed a more hospitable attitude toward new scientific theories. Accordingly, he resumed his pro-Copernican activities. In 1632 he published his *Dialogue of the Two Great Systems of the World,* a thinly disguised defense of the Copernican theory. The sale of the book was prohibited, and its author was summoned to Rome by the Inquisition. Examined under threat of torture, he recanted and denied that he held Copernican opinions. He was, nevertheless, condemned as "vehemently suspected of heresy" and sentenced to be incarcerated at the pleasure of the Inquisition. After six months he was permitted to return to Florence to spend the remaining eight years of his life in strict seclusion.

Like Galileo, Giordano Bruno was a Copernican and an opponent of the Aristotelian conception of the universe. He ran afoul of the Church, however, not for his scientific views but for his ethics and metaphysics. (*See Reading No. 8D.*) He taught that men should be judged for their deeds and not according to their belief in this or that catechism or creed. He scoffed at the mysteries of the Christian faith, ridiculed miracles as magical tricks, and put the Jewish records on a level with the Greek and Roman myths. Fundamentally, he was a pantheist, who believed in a universe governed by immutable laws. He, therefore, taught the uselessness of prayer and denied the conception of a providential God who sets the course of nature aside for the benefit of some of His creatures. By following a wandering life from one European refuge to another, Bruno escaped the blood-hounds of the Inquisition for more than fifteen years. But eventually they overtook him in Venice in 1593. He was thrown into prison and spent seven years in confinement. On the ninth of February, 1600 he was formally condemned and on the seventeenth was burned at the stake.

Witchcraft Persecutions. The witchcraft persecutions of the sixteenth and seventeenth centuries may also be regarded as examples of the bigotry and fanaticism generated by the Reformation. The dreary record of superstition, tortures, and executions is almost too well known to deserve recounting here. During the period referred to at least 30,000 persons were put to death for the alleged crime of entering into compacts with Satan. As the theologians defined it, witchcraft consisted in selling one's soul to the devil in return for supernatural powers. It was held that a person who had made such a bargain was thereby enabled to work all manner of spiteful magic against other people —to cause their cattle to sicken and die, their crops to fail, or their children to fall into the fire. But the most valuable gifts bestowed by Satan were the power to blind husbands to their wives' misconduct or to cause women to give birth to idiotic or deformed infants. It has been commonly assumed that the so-called witches were toothless old hags whose cranky habits and venomous tongues had made them objects of suspicion and dread to all who knew them. Undoubtedly, a great many of the victims, especially in America, did belong to this class. European writers, however, generally imagined the witch to be a "fair and wicked young woman," and a large percentage of those put to death in Germany and France were adolescent girls and matrons not yet thirty.

Persecutions for witchcraft seem to have begun with the crusades launched against the Albigenses by the Papal Inquisition in the thirteenth century. A second campaign against witches was initiated in 1484 by Pope Innocent VIII, who instructed his inquisitors to use torture in procuring convictions. But it was not until after the beginning of the Reformation that witchcraft persecution became a mad hysteria. Luther himself provided some of the impetus by recommending that witches should be put to death with fewer considerations of mercy than were shown to ordinary criminals. Other Reformers quickly followed Luther's example. Under Calvin's administration in Geneva thirty-four women were burned or quartered for the alleged crime in 1545. Women, young girls, and even mere children were tortured by driving needles under their nails, roasting their feet in the fire, or crushing their legs under heavy weights until the marrow spurted from their bones, in order to force them to confess filthy orgies with demons. To what extent the persecutions were the result of sheer sadism or the greed of magistrates, who were sometimes permitted to confiscate the property of those convicted, is impossible to say. Certainly there were few people who did not believe in the reality of witchcraft or did not consider the burning of its practitioners justifiable. Sir Francis Bacon contributed his endorsement of the superstition, and apparently Shakespeare took witchcraft for granted. One of the most vigorous defenders of the trials and executions was the political philosopher Jean Bodin, whose zeal earned for him the appellation, "Satan's Attorney-General." (*See Reading No. 8C.*)

It is a noteworthy fact that protests against persecutions for witchcraft came not from theologians but almost exclusively from laymen, some of them quite unorthodox in religion. In 1584 an English jurist, Reginald Scott, published a book condemning the belief in witchcraft as irrational and asserting that most of the lurid crimes confessed by accused women were figments of disordered minds. Such eminent scientists as Pierre Gassendi and William Harvey also denounced the persecutions. But the most effective protest of all came from the pen of Montaigne. This distinguished essayist and skeptic directed the shafts of his most powerful ridicule against the preposterous nonsense of the sorcery trials and the cruelty of men like Bodin who would have had witches killed on mere suspicion. That the religious leaders showed almost no interest in abating or terminating the witchcraft mania is not easy to understand. Of course, they were confronted by the injunc-

tion in the Old Testament, "Thou shalt not suffer a witch
to live," but as Christians they were supposed to give pre-
eminence to the humane and gentle gospel of Jesus. Leaders of the Catholic Reformation failed to take advantage
of what would seem to have been a good opportunity to
cut some of the ground from under the Protestant secession. They might well have indicted Protestantism as an
Old Testament religion and have demonstrated a connection between its zeal for the persecution of witches and its
morbid doctrines of original sin and the total depravity of
human nature. Instead, they showed as fiery an ardor for
dealing unmercifully with so-called witches as did Lutherans or Calvinists.

Intolerance and persecution were not confined, of course,
to individuals. Though Protestants did not burn Catholics,
conceding that the Roman Church was the repository of
the core of Christianity, they did make life intolerable for
them in territories they managed to control. Catholics, on
the other hand, regarded all Protestants as heretics and
therefore entitled to no mercy at the hands of the Church.
Nevertheless, in some cases Catholic leaders were quite
willing to tolerate the more conservative Protestants. After
the rise of the Anabaptists, for example, the followers of
Luther came to be recognized as a welcome defense against
anarchy and civil disorder. By the Peace of Augsburg
(1555) the Catholic majority agreed that each German
prince should decide for himself whether the religion of
his subjects should be Lutheran or Catholic. Actually, both
Catholics and Protestants tended to concentrate their intolerance upon the extremist groups rather than upon each
other. Especially Anabaptists and anti-Trinitarians bore the
brunt of orthodox savagery from every direction. No doubt
this was inevitable, since such groups were considered as
undermining not merely religion but the foundations of the
social order as well.

Other Examples of Intolerance and Fanaticism.   The
repressive activities of the Inquisition and of the Congregation of the Index must also be classified under the bigotry
and fanaticism of the Catholic Reformation. The same is
true of the wars for the liquidation of Protestants in Ger-

many, in the Low Countries, and in France. Moreover, most of these wars had political rather than purely religious objectives. The Holy Roman Emperor could use the excuse, at least, that Central Europe was threatened by the Turks, and that the Empire could not afford to be weakened by religious dissension within its borders. The kings of France longed for unity at home in order to advance their schemes in Central and Southern Europe, while King Philip II regarded the rebellion of his Protestant subjects in the Low Countries as a nuisance standing in the way of his ambition to achieve dominance over the whole Continent. It is noteworthy that the settlements of at least two of these wars conformed more closely to political than to religious considerations. The Schmalkaldic War waged by Charles V in an effort to stamp out Lutheranism in Germany ended in the compromise Peace of Augsburg, under which each German prince would have the right to choose either Lutheranism or Catholicism as the faith of his people. (*See Reading No. 7A.*) The war against the Huguenots in France was brought to an end by the Edict of Nantes in 1598, which granted freedom of conscience to both Huguenots and Catholics. In issuing this edict, King Henry IV was not actuated by religious liberalism. Indeed, he cared little about religion, as is evidenced by the fact that he changed his allegiance from Protestant to Catholic in order to obtain the French crown. His sole motive in granting religious freedom to his people was to bring peace to a distracted kingdom. He considered political unity much more important than creedal uniformity. (*See Reading No. 7B.*)

Political Results: Absolutism vs. Limited Government. The political attitudes of the Catholic Reformation showed an even greater divergence than did those of the Protestant Revolution. Both Protestants and Catholics wavered between support of absolute government and endorsement of the right of rebellion. The explanation is not far to seek. According to the Apostle Paul and most of his successors among the Church Fathers, government was a divinely established institution. The powers that be were ordained of God, and anyone who resisted the civil powers resisted the ordinance of God. The last of the Church Fathers, Gregory the Great, taught that even a tyrant must be obeyed, no matter how oppressive his rule might become; for tyranny was better than sin, and the fact that God had appointed a tyrant to rule over a people was a sure sign that they needed a harsh regime as a corrective and preventive of sin. With the development of a variety of religions, however, the problem was no longer so simple. Suppose the ruler persecuted the followers of the "true" religion, or sought to establish some "false" gospel in which a large minority, or perhaps the majority, of his subjects did not believe. Were they obligated to obey him and submit to his rule over them as their divinely appointed sovereign? Some Calvinists sought a compromise solution by asserting the right of "inferior magistrates" to oppose and even to depose such a ruler. This doctrine was suggested by Calvin himself and by his associate, Theodore Beza. It was made more explicit by the French Huguenots, especially by the authors of the *Vindiciae contra Tyrannos,* published in 1579. From this doctrine it was not a difficult step to asserting that the people, acting through a majority, may exercise the right of rebellion against an unjust or unlawful ruler, and that in case of dire need any one of their number may put him to death. Such was the view enunciated by George Buchanan in connection with the revolt of the Scottish Calvinists against their Catholic queen.

The cleavage in Catholic attitudes was more sharply cut. In general, the Church lent its support to absolute political rule. The Popes themselves ruled despotically over the States of the Church. The Council of Trent legislated on almost every conceivable subject, but it had nothing to say regarding the right of the people to protection against tyrants and unjust princes. Throughout the Reformation period the hierarchy supported the policies of those sovereigns who favored the Church regardless of how greedy they might be for power and plunder at their subjects' expense. The views of the Jesuits, however, stood out in bold contrast to the attitudes of the Church in general. The cardinal aim of the Jesuits was to revivify the theory of papal superiority in accordance with the medieval pattern developed by Gregory VII, Innocent III, and Boniface VIII. They hoped to restore not only the supremacy of the Pope in all matters clearly related to religion but to reestablish the position of the Church as an international organization with a higher authority than any national state. They dreamed of accomplishing this aim by conceding to the national governments independence in secular affairs in return for recognition of the spiritual leadership of the Pope over a society of Christian states. The collapse of this dream was largely a result of the failure of the Jesuits to realize the strength of the hold which nationalism had taken upon the minds not only of Protestants but of tens of thousands of Catholics.

Bellarmine. Jesuit political theory was first elaborated, though not in its highest form, by Robert Bellarmine (1542-1621), the renowned Italian Cardinal and controversialist of the sixteenth century. Though commonly regarded as the champion *par excellence* of the papacy, Bellarmine denied that the Pope has any direct authority over secular matters. But he does have an indirect authority exclusively for spiritual ends. Bellarmine's argument for this conclusion was as follows: The power of secular rulers does not come from God or even from the Pope. Instead, it derives from the people themselves for the sake of their own secular welfare. No prince can therefore have absolute power to command his subjects regardless of their good. Bellarmine did not set up any effective check upon the exercise of such arbitrary power, save in one particular. That particular was the case of an heretical ruler. Because the authority of the Pope comes directly from God and is therefore unquestionable in all spiritual matters, the Roman pontiff may depose an heretical ruler and absolve his subjects from their allegiance. From this conclusion Bellarmine went on to argue that the Pope may exercise a general control over secular rulers, always of course, for "spiritual" purposes. Except for the element of the popular origin of royal power, Bellarmine's theory closely paralleled the doctrines of medieval papalists from the eleventh to the fourteenth century.

Suarez. The most original of the Jesuit political thinkers was the Spanish philosopher and jurist Francisco Suarez (1548-1617). He agreed with most of the premises and conclusions of Bellarmine, though he defined them more clearly. In common with the Italian Cardinal, he taught that political power comes from the people, and that it exists for the common welfare. It can never be absolute, since the needs of the community are not constant but variable. When political power no longer contributes to the welfare of the community, it can be changed, just as the government itself may be changed for the public good. Suarez agreed also with Bellarmine that the power of the Pope comes from God. Both men denied the divine right of kings partly in order to exalt the divine authority of the Pope. They conceived of the Roman pontiff as not simply the head of a church but as the spiritual ruler of a family of Christian nations and therefore as the arbiter of the moral interests of humanity. They regarded the Church as a great international organization and the various national states as simply its local members.

The most original element in Suarez' philosophy was his development of a theory of law. (*See Reading No. 8E.*) He argued that in human nature and in relations among human beings there are certain considerations that make some forms of conduct unquestionably right and others unquestionably wrong. For example, nothing could make deliberate murder of another human being right or kindness and benevolence wrong. Such forms of behavior are right or wrong by a higher law of nature which even the Pope cannot change, much less any secular ruler. Suarez seemed to imply that God Himself would be powerless to veto or to set aside the law of nature. Since states no less than individuals are bound by this law, Suarez envisioned it as an essential ingredient in a code for regulating the relations among nations. His contribution to the development of international law in the sixteenth and seventeenth centuries was therefore substantial.

Mariana. The most radical of the Jesuit political theorists was the Spanish philosopher Juan de Mariana (1535?-1623). Indeed, his teachings were so heterodox that he can hardly be considered a typical Jesuit. Two of his tracts were placed on the Index, and he was imprisoned for a time by the Inquisition. Nevertheless, he remained a member of the Society of Jesus from the age of seventeen until his death at the age of eighty-eight. He was recognized as a talented expositor of the philosophy of Thomas Aquinas, and he taught theology in Jesuit schools in Sicily, in Paris, and in Rome. Mariana's theory of politics was almost entirely non-theological. He said little about the spiritual authority of the Pope and apparently did not recognize papal superiority over civil rulers. He expounded a theory of constitutionalism medieval in origin but completely secular. He conceived of government arising from a pre-political state of nature. As Rousseau did later, he taught that this animal existence was brought to an end by the origin of private property. This made men avaricious and aggressive and necessitated the development of agencies for social control. He limited these agencies to a monarch and the Estates of the realm. The Estates would consist of the chief members of the various classes and would be the guardians of the law of the land. This law was not natural law but a kind of embodiment of long-standing customs regarded as occupying a higher plane than statutes and edicts. Only the Estates could change this fundamental law, and they would have the power to depose a king who violated it. Mariana was so determined to impose restraints upon high-handed monarchs that he frankly endorsed tyrannicide, even when committed by a private citizen, provided only that there was sufficient cause in the form of oppression or injustice to warrant it.

Not all Catholic political thought during the Reformation period was Jesuit. Some members of the faith espoused both nationalism and despotism in contradistinction to the internationalism and anti-absolutism of the Jesuits. Characteristic of non-Jesuit Catholic thought were the teachings of the so-called *Politiques*. Confined primarily to France, the *Politiques* subordinated religion to politics. Some were so completely secular in outlook that it was almost impossible to tell whether they were Catholics,

Protestants, or atheists. Their cardinal objectives were domestic peace and unity in order that the state might grow strong and fulfill its true mission to its people. If religion interfered with these objectives, then so much the worse for religion. The *Politiques* took the same attitude toward parties. Any form of sectarianism or partisan contention they abhorred as a threat to the unity of the state. Though mostly professing Catholics, they were nationalists above everything else. They resented any efforts to enforce conformity of religious beliefs upon persons who would not accept them voluntarily, and they excoriated attempts to subordinate the state in any way to the papal authority in Rome. They argued that the division of Christianity was an irreparable fact, and that the theologians' hope for a universal church was an idle dream. They condemned religious persecution, therefore, not on moral but on utilitarian grounds: it would be ruinous to the state. For purposes of maintaining peace and unity they also approved of strong government. They regarded the king as the personification of the state and looked askance at any provisions for reducing or restraining his power.

Jean Bodin.   The political philosophy of Jean Bodin (1530-1596) resembled so closely that of the *Politiques* that he might almost be considered a member of that school. In any case his theories were clearly a product of the Catholic Reformation. Like the *Politiques,* he adopted as his objective the preservation of order and unity in the state. (*See Reading No. 8F.*) To accomplish this aim he proposed to exalt the prince above all sects and parties and to deny his subjection to any external authority. He agreed with the medieval philosophers that rulers were bound by the law of God, and he acknowledged that the prince had a moral duty to respect the treaties he had signed. But he had no use for parliaments of any description. He emphatically denied the right of a legislative body to impose any limits on royal power. And while he admitted that princes who violated the divine law or the law of nature were tyrants, he refused to concede that their subjects had any right of rebellion against them. The supreme obligation of the people is passive obedience. Revolution must be avoided at all costs, for it destroys that stability which is a necessary condition for progress.

The most original contribution of Bodin was his doctrine of sovereignty, which he defined as "supreme power over citizens and subjects, unrestrained by the laws." By this he meant that the prince, who is the only sovereign, is not bound by man-made laws. He is subject to no *legal* restriction whatever—nothing except a *moral* obligation to obey the law of nature and the law of God. Bodin is significant also for his theory of the origin of the state. Rejecting the old feudal doctrine of the contractual basis of political authority, he maintained that the state was an outgrowth of the patriarchal family. The prince stands in the same autocratic relation to his subjects as the father does to his children. This contention represented a repudiation of the limited government theories of the High Middle Ages, and it prepared the way for justification of the blatant despotism of later monarchs.

Education and Culture. That the Reformation would have significant effects upon education goes almost without saying. Every one of the various sects recognized the importance of schools as instruments of indoctrination. While they feared intellectual influences as sources of skepticism and infidelity, they believed that schools properly organized and managed would have nothing but beneficial effects. Luther declared that "Good schools are the tree from which grow all good conduct in life, and if they decay great blindness must follow in religion and in all useful arts." Repeatedly he urged the civil authorities to "compel people to send their children to school." John Calvin praised learning as "a public necessity to secure good political administration, sustain the Church unharmed and maintain humanity among men." As for the Catholic Reformation attitude, the devotion of the Jesuits to thorough and effective instruction is so well known as to require no comment.

The influence of the Reformation upon education was mixed and varied. Some aspects of it were undoubtedly good. The Protestant Reformers broke through the aristocratic system that had come down from the Renaissance

and sponsored education for the masses. Both Luther and
Calvin recommended that schools be maintained at public
expense for the children of all classes, rich and poor, high
and low. Luther insisted also that the schools provide
vocational training for those who were not of outstanding
intellectual ability. Though he did not completely reject
the humanistic education of the Renaissance, he demanded
more attention to useful and practical subjects. Calvin,
strangely enough, was less radical. Though he established
a system of elementary education in the vernacular for
all, based upon thorough instruction in reading, writing,
arithmetic, and grammar, he also organized secondary
schools, or *colleges,* to prepare leaders for the ministry
and for government service. The curriculum in these colleges did not depart widely from the usual humanistic one.

The most systematic activities on behalf of educational
reform in the sixteenth and seventeenth centuries were
those of the Catholics. The Jesuits especially gained an
enviable reputation for the quality of their schools. These
were *colleges* exclusively, "lower" colleges or secondary
schools, and "upper" colleges or universities. The Jesuits
did not engage in elementary education. They required
that their students already possess a knowledge of the
rudimentary subjects before being admitted to any school.
As with the Lutherans and the Calvinists, their schools
were essentially democratic. No tuition fees were charged,
and generally speaking, the poor and humble mingled
indiscriminately with the wealthy and aristocratic. The
curriculum in the lower colleges was a mixture of religion
and humanistic studies. The latter comprised primarily
speaking and writing Ciceronian Latin, though in the final
years some study of Greek was introduced. Except on holi-
days no word of a vernacular language could ever be used.
In the upper colleges the curriculum was broadened to include the study of Hebrew and other Oriental languages,
church history, canon law, theology, and above all, philosophy. The last embraced not merely logic, metaphysics,
and ethics, but mathematics and some of the new sciences
such as physics, chemistry, astronomy, and physiology.
The Jesuits had perhaps the most thorough system of

teacher training of any of the sects of the Reformation period. No one could teach in a lower college who had not completed the philosophical course which led to the degree of Master of Arts. For teachers in the upper colleges the usual requirement was completion of the theological course of six years for the degree of Doctor of Divinity.

In addition to the Society of Jesus the Catholic Reformation gave rise to some other teaching orders. Among these were the Order of Ursulines, founded in 1535; the Congregation of Christian Doctrine, founded in 1592; the Sisters of Notre Dame, started in 1598; and the Piarists, established in 1597. All of these orders engaged in elementary education exclusively. Some, like the Sisters of Notre Dame, devoted themselves to the training of girls, especially in such practical arts as sewing. All of them were concerned primarily with the education of children of the poor. A typical example was the Piarists, whose first school was opened in Rome, in 1597, by a Spanish priest who was appalled by the lack of educational opportunities for the sons of laborers and craftsmen. He established an order patterned in methods and organization after the model of the Jesuits. It extended its activities especially into the border lands of Italy and Germany. Mention of the organized teaching orders is not to overlook the activities of the older agencies of the Church, notably in the cathedral cities. In Paris, for example, the Archbishop organized a complete system of elementary schools, with teachers licensed by the Precentor of Notre Dame. Instruction was provided to children of the laboring classes, of both sexes, in reading, writing, arithmetic, Latin, grammar, Catechism, and singing.

We cannot look upon all the educational effects of the Reformation and pronounce them good. For one thing, the anti-intellectualism of most of the reformers could not have had other than a deleterious influence. Luther described the universities as "great gates of Hell" and "dens of murderers"; he referred to Aristotle as a "damnable heathen" and to human reason as "the Devil's harlot." He did, it is true, exert some efforts on behalf of humanistic studies, and he called the neglect of languages "a disgrace and a sin." His motive, however, was purely religious. The study of Greek and Latin literature would strengthen knowledge of the ancient languages, and these were necessary to "preserve the Scriptures." Ignatius of Loyola, in his *Spiritual Exercises,* enjoined his followers to "lay aside all private judgment" and to obey in all things the "hierarchical Church." They must always be ready to believe that what seemed to them white was black, if the "hierarchical Church" so defined it. It seems obvious that the common people could not go long unaffected by the anti-intellectual diatribes of their leaders. Some had already begun to distrust learning because of the overemphasis by Renaissance educators upon "useless" and "impractical" studies. Now with the blasts of the reformers against it, the work of the schools seemed ever more useless and even wicked. The Scriptures, they were told, were the real guide to life and truth. Why, then, should one waste precious years on the intricacies of Latin grammar and the heresies and obscenities of heathen writers?

The baneful effects of the Reformation are graphically illustrated by the figures on the decline of the universities. In 1516, the year before the beginning of the Protestant Revolt, the University of Cologne had 370 students; eight years later it had fifty-four. In 1521 the University of Leipzig enrolled 340 students; in 1526, eighty-one. The University of Rostock, the leading educational center of northern Germany, saw its enrollment dwindle from about 300 before the Protestant Revolt to fifteen in 1525, and to zero in 1529. At Luther's own University of Wittenberg there were 245 students in 1521 and only seventy-three six years later. It has been alleged that these declines were caused by the overthrow of the Catholic Church in northern Germany and the consequent elimination of thousands of opportunities for employment for university graduates in ecclesiastical positions. But the decline of the universities was not confined to northern Germany. Conditions were not much different in those areas that remained loyal, or were won back after a few years to Mother Church.

Erfurt, the principal seat of humanistic learning in Germany, enrolled 311 students during the year 1520-1521, but only fourteen six years later. The University of Vienna declined from 661 new matriculants in 1519 to twelve in 1532. In fairness it should be added that both Protestants and Catholics established new universities during the later years of the sixteenth century. By this time both the suspicion of learning as an instrument of the devil and the turmoil of sectarian strife had partially subsided. Among the noted Protestant institutions were the universities of Zürich, Geneva, Edinburgh, Leyden, and Jena. New Catholic foundations included nine universities in Spain and four in Italy.

The effect of the Reformation on intellect and the arts did not differ greatly from that on education. Dogmatism, the subordination of learning to the uses of orthodoxy, the encouragement of superstitions like witchcraft and the belief in demons, anti-intellectualism, repression, and fanaticism provided an environment distinctly inhospitable to nearly all forms of cultural progress. Yet some progress did occur. Political theory flowered for a time, as is usually the case, under the stimulus of controversy. The period of the Catholic Reformation was an age of considerable advancement in science, especially in Italy. The anatomists Fabricius, Vesalius, and Harvey and the astronomers Copernicus and Galileo did their work in that country, and not always with hindrance from the church. The Copernican theory, for example, was approved at first by Pope Clement VII.

In the realm of the fine arts the Reformation exerted, perhaps, its most beneficent influence upon music. The Catholic Reformation conditioned and stimulated the work of the great Palestrina. The restraint, dignity, and moods of devout meditation expressed in his masses and motets exemplify the highest standards of religious dedication. He received pensions and awards from several Popes, and he was appointed composer to the Sistine Chapel. Yet his reputation had a narrow escape. In 1562 the Council of Trent condemned the prevailing style of ecclesiastical music

as too sensuous. As a consequence, the ascetic Pope Paul
IV seriously considered eliminating all music from Church
services except monophonic and the unaccompanied plain
chant. A special investigating commission, however, approved Palestrina's music and thereby saved the Roman
Church from imitating the ridiculous example of the Calvinists in forbidding instrumental music entirely. Another
composer, Orlandus Lassus, contributed almost as much
to the richness and variety of sixteenth-century music as
did Palestrina. A Belgian by birth, Lassus worked not for
Popes but for the Dukes of Bavaria. Much of his music,
therefore, was secular and even ribald and hilarious. Yet
no one excelled him in his dedication to the sublime. He
was a friend of high dignitaries of the Church and at one
time held an appointment at the Church of St. John Lateran
in Rome.

The influence of the Reformation on the so-called arts
of design was, for the most part, adverse. None of the
Protestant leaders cared anything about painting or sculp-
ture, and Calvin, at least, considered them pagan and immoral. He demanded the elimination of all paintings and
statues from the churches in order that the attention of
worshipers might not be diverted by appeals to their senses.
The stern asceticism of the reform Popes was shocked by
the realism of some of the art objects collected from pagan
sources by their predecessors of the Renaissance period.
But some of the works of their own time provoked a similar
hostility. The Council of Trent issued stern decrees against
nude pictures and sponsored the employment of a second-
rate artist to paint breeches and skirts on the naked figures
in Michelangelo's *Last Judgment*. Even in its attempts to
encourage a new art compatible with the beliefs of the
Church, the Catholic Reformation did almost as much
damage to aesthetic standards as it had done by its hostility to the old. Painting took on qualities of sentimentality
and insincerity. Architecture became grandiose and osten-
tatious. Though some splendid monuments, exemplified by
St. Peter's Basilica in Rome, were created, scarcely any
possessed the charm and originality that distinguished the

Gothic cathedrals of the Middle Ages or the great structures of the early Renaissance.

In the perspective of history, the Catholic Reformation, along with its Protestant counterpart, was the culmination of a series of religious reform movements that went back to the tenth century. The series began with the Cluny movement and included the Cistercian, Carthusian, Franciscan, and Waldensian movements. A little later came the Conciliar movement and the Christian Renaissance. Some of these movements were at least partly successful. Others attempted too much or encountered such strong opposition that failure was their inevitable portion. All had the same purpose: to restore some golden age of the past when goodness and simplicity prevailed over corruption, greed, and injustice. Had the Catholic Reformation fulfilled its destiny, it would have sought to restore the Christian religion to its medieval foundations, to revive the ideals of rationalism, tolerance, limited government, and universalism that had made the thirteenth century in some respects the "greatest of centuries." Instead, the Catholic leaders allowed themselves to become embroiled in controversies with their Protestant opponents over such relatively minor issues as "communion in both kinds," auricular confession, and the invocation of saints. The bitterness engendered by such controversies prevented both phases of the Reformation from contributing in any major degree to the liberation of man.

Part II

SELECTED READINGS

Within the readings that follow, a number of footnotes and references have been deleted because of space limitations. The reader is urged to consult the sources cited.

THE CHRISTIAN RENAISSANCE

The Christian Renaissance is almost synonymous with northern humanism. At least, it found typical expression in the writings of such celebrated humanists as Johann Reuchlin, Desiderius Erasmus, and Sir Thomas More. Their methods were not those of radical dogmatism or violent change but rather of irony, tolerance, and appeals to reason. The first of the examples that follow is from The Letters of Obscure Men, *in which friends of Johann Reuchlin attempt by ridicule to lay bare some common superstitions. The second example is an abridgment of Erasmus'* Enchiridion, *or* Handbook of a Christian Knight. *In it the Prince of the Humanists emphasizes the importance of knowledge as well as devoutness in the practice of religion. The third document illustrates how the political philosophy of Erasmus was interwoven with his religious ideals. "To be a philosopher and to be a Christian," he says, "is synonymous in fact." In the final extract Sir Thomas More presents an eloquent statement of his philosophy of religious toleration.*

✓   ✓   ✓

A.
Example of the Letters of Obscure Men*

Henricus Schaffsmulius, to Master Ortuinus Gratius, many salutations.

* University of Pennsylvania, *Translations and Reprints from the Original Sources of European History* (Philadelphia, 1897), vol. II, pp. 3-4.

When I first went to the Curia you told me that I should write to you frequently and address any theological questions to you, for you wished to answer them more satisfactorily than those about the Papal Court at Rome. I, therefore, wish now to ask your opinion in the case of one who should on Friday, which is the sixth day, or upon any other fast day, eat an egg in which there was a chick. For we were recently dining at an inn in the Campo Fiore and were eating eggs. And I, opening my egg, discovered that there was a chick within; but upon showing it to my companion, he urged me to swallow it straightway before the host caught sight of it, for otherwise I should have to pay a Carolinus or a Julius for a fowl, since it is the custom here to pay for everything the host places upon the table, because they will take nothing back. Now if he saw that there was a chick in the egg, he would say: "You must pay me for a fowl too, for he would charge for a little one just as much as he would for a big one."

And I immediately swallowed the egg and the chick at the same time, and afterwards it occurred to me that it was Friday, and I said to my companion: "You have caused me to commit a mortal sin in eating meat on the sixth day."

But he said that it was not a mortal sin, nor even a venial sin, since a chick may not be considered other than egg until it is born. And he remarked that it is just so in the case of cheese, in which there are worms, and of those in cherries, and in peas, and young beans, but they are eaten on the sixth day and even on the vigils of the Apostles. But inn proprietors are such rascals, they say that these are meat in order to make gain thereby.

Then I went out and thought about it, and by Heaven, Master Ortwin, I am much disturbed, and I do not know what I ought to do about it. It is true that I might take counsel with a member of the Papal Court, but I know that they have bad consciences. As for myself, it seems to me that chicks in the egg are meat, because the matter is already formed and shaped into the members and body of an animal, and it has animal life. It is otherwise in the case of worms in cheese and other comestibles, for worms are accounted to be fish, as I have heard from a physician, who is also a very able scientist.

I beseech of you earnestly to reply to my question. For if you hold that it is a mortal sin, then I wish to seek absolution before I go to Germany; for you probably know that our lord, Jacob Hochstraten, borrowed a thousand florins from the bank, and I believe he would want to make something out of the case, and may the devil take that John Reuchlin and those other poets and men of law, who are trying to fight the Church of God,—that is to say, the theologians, who are the real backbone of the Church, as Christ said: "Thou art Peter, and upon this rock will I build my Church."

May the Lord God preserve you. Farewell.
Written in the City of Rome.

B.

Erasmus, Enchiridion*

The Second Chapter. What Means are to be Used in the War of a Christian Man

WHEREAS nothing pertaineth more to the war of a christian man, than to know with what weapons he must fight, and to have the same always ready at hand; even so, considering the adversary is never idle, we ought not to cease from war; but if we will fight against the multitude of vices, we ought always to watch, to have our mind armed, and to take the weapons of defence; but specially to provide us of two, namely, prayer and knowledge, which be the chief armour of a christian man. Perfect prayer lifteth up the mind unto God; knowledge armeth the mind with wholesome precepts and honest opinions. These two cleave so together, that the one cannot lack the other: for as the one maketh intercession, so the other teacheth how we ought to pray, namely, in the name of Jesu; and what we ought to desire, even that which is wholesome for our

* Abridgment of the *Enchiridion* of Erasmus. From Myles Coverdale, *Writings and Translations* (Cambridge: The University Press, 1844), pp. 497-98.

soul's health. Now though prayer be more excellent, because she talketh familiarly with Almighty God, yet is knowledge no less necessary: which as it ought not to be imperfect, so ought not prayer to be faint, slack, or without quickness; neither can we well perform the great journey that we have to go, without the aid and help of these two means. The use of prayer is not to mumble and babble much, as they do that are not ripe in God's Spirit. For five words spoken in knowledge are better than ten thousand babbled with the mouth. Neither is it the noise of our lips, but the fervent desire of the mind, that God alloweth. Which fervent prayer, with like study or meditation of the holy scripture, is able as well to put aback the great violence of our enemies, as to make easy our grievous adversity. If we with this heavenly manna and food of God be refreshed in the furtherance of our journey, it shall make us bold and strong to buckle with our enemies. For the doctrine of God, as it only is pure and undefiled, contrary to the nature of men's doctrines; even so to them that, spiritually understanding it, may abide the hearing thereof, there is nothing sweeter nor more pleasant, and therefore the more worthy to be searched and well pondered. This is the river of comfort, the fountain of ease, the well that refresheth the weary, the water of Siloe, where the blind receive their sight: to the study whereof if we apply ourselves wholly, that is, if we exercise our minds continually in the law of God, we shall be so armed, that we need not to fear any assault of our enemies.

C.

Erasmus, The Education of a Christian Prince*

Death is not to be feared, nor should we wail when it comes to others, unless it was a foul death. The happiest man is not the one who has lived the longest, but the one who has made the most of his life. The span of life should be measured not by years but by our deeds well performed.

* Translated by L. K. Born (New York: Columbia University Press, 1936), pp. 149-50.

Length of life has no bearing on a man's happiness. It is
how well he lived that counts. Surely virtue is its own
reward. It is the duty of a good prince to consider the
welfare of his people, even at the cost of his own life if
need be. But that prince does not really die who loses his
life in such a cause. All those things which the common
people cherish as delightful, or revere as excellent, or
adopt as useful, are to be measured by just one standard
—worth. On the other hand, whatever things the common
people object to as disagreeable, or despise as lowly, or
shun as pernicious, should not be avoided unless they
are bound up with dishonor.

These principles should be fixed in the mind of the
future prince. They should be impressed in his tender
young heart as the most hallowed laws, *les lois les plus
sacrées*. Let him hear many being praised for these ideas
and others reprimanded for diverse ones. Then he will be
accustomed from the start to expect praise as a result of
good things and to abhor the ignominy that comes from
the opposite. But here some one of those frumps at the
court, more stupid and worthless than any woman you
could name, will interrupt with this: "You are making us
a philosopher, not a prince." "I am making a prince," I
answer, "although you prefer a worthless sot like yourself instead of a real prince!" You cannot be a prince, if
you are not a philosopher; you will be a tyrant. There is
nothing better than a good prince. A tyrant is such a mon-
strous beast that his like does not exist. Nothing is equally
baneful, nothing more hateful to all. Do not think that
Plato rashly advanced the idea, which was lauded by the
most praiseworthy men, that the blessed state will be that
in which the princes are philosophers, or in which the
philosophers seize the principate. I do not mean by philosopher, one who is learned in the ways of dialectic or
physics, but one who casts aside the false pseudo-realities
and with open mind seeks and follows the truth. To be a
philosopher and to be a Christian is synonymous in fact.
The only difference is in the nomenclature.

What is more stupid than to judge a prince on the following accomplishments: his ability to dance gracefully, dice

expertly, drink with a gusto, swell with pride, plunder the people with kingly grandeur, and do all the other things which I am ashamed even to mention, although there are plenty who are not ashamed to do them? The common run of princes zealously avoid the dress and manner of living of the lower classes. Just so should the true prince be removed from the sullied opinions and desires of the common folk. The one thing which he should consider base, vile, and unbecoming to him is to share the opinions of the common people who never are interested in anything worth while. How ridiculous it is for one adorned with gems, gold, the royal purple, attended by courtiers, possessing all the other marks of honor, wax images and statues, wealth that clearly is not his, to be so far superior to all because of them, and yet in the light of real goodness of spirit to be found inferior to many born from the very dregs of society.

D.
Sir Thomas More, Utopia*

. . . For kyng Utopus, even at the firste beginning, hearing that the inhabitauntes of the land wer, before his comming thether, at continuall dissention and strife amonge themselves for their religions; perceyving also that this common dissention (whiles every severall secte tooke several partes in fighting for their countrey) was the only occasion of his conquest over them al, as sone as he had gotten the victory, firste of all he made a decree, that it should be lawfull for everie man to favoure and folow what religion he would, and that he mighte do the best he could to bring other to his opinion, so that he did it peaceablie, gentelie, quietly and soberlie, without hastie and contentious rebuking and invehing against other. If he could not by faire and gentle speche induce them unto his opinion yet he should use no kinde of violence, and refraine from displeasaunte and seditious woordes. To him

* Translated by Raphe Robynson (Cambridge: The University Press, 1890), pp. 146-47.

that would vehemently and ferventlye in this cause strive
and contende was decreed banishment or bondage. This
lawe did kynge Utopus make not only for the maintenance of peace, which he saw through continuall contention
and mortal hatred utterly extinguished; but also because he
thought this decrie should make for the furtheraunce of
religion. Whereof he durst define and determine nothing
unadvisedlie, as douting whether God desiering manifolde
and diverse sortes of honour, would inspire sondry men
with sondrie kindes of religion. And this suerly he thought
a very unmete and folish thing, and a point of arrogant
presumption, to compell all other by violence and threaten-
inges to agre to the same that thou belevest to be trew.
Furthermore thoughe there be one religion whiche alone
is trew, and al other vaine and superstitious, yet did he wel
foresee (so that the matter were handeled with reason,
and sober modestie) that the trueth of the own powre
would at the last issue out and come to lyghte. But if
contention and debate in that behalfe should continuallye
be used, as the woorste men be mooste obstinate and stub-
bourne, and in their evyll opinion mooste constante; he
perceaved that then the beste and holyest religion woulde be
troden underfote and destroyed by most vaine supersticions,
even as good corne is by thornes and weedes overgrowen
and chooked. Therfore all this matter he lefte undiscussed,
and gave to everye man free libertie and choise to beleve
what he woulde. Savinge that he earnestelye and straitelye
charged them, that no man should conceave so vile and
baase an opinion of the dignitie of mans nature, as to think
that the soules do die and perishe with the bodye; or that
the world runneth at al aventures governed by no divine
providence. And therfore thei beleve that after this life
vices be extreamelye punished and vertues bountifully
rewarded. Hym that is of a contrary opinion they counte
not in the numbre of men, as one that hathe avaled the
heighe nature of hys soule to the vielnes of brute beastes
bodies, muche lesse in the numbre of their citiziens, whose
lawes and ordenaunces, if it were not for feare, he wold
nothing at al esteme . . .

— Reading No. 2 —

MYSTICISM

Mysticism is the belief that the supreme good for man is oneness with God or the divine essence, that God can be apprehended not by reason or the intellect but only by insight or intuition, and that union with Him can be effected by visions, trances, self-denial, or self-inflicted suffering. Mysticism contributed an important part to the Reformation, in both its Protestant and Catholic phases. The founder of Christian mysticism was St. Bernard of Clairvaux (1091-1153). Mystics who influenced the course of the Reformation included Meister Eckhart (1260?-1327), Thomas à Kempis (1380-1471), and St. Teresa (1515-1582).

✓　　　✓　　　✓

A.
From the Sermons of Meister Eckhart*

. . . one must be so dead to all that is personal, that he could be as fond of persons long dead as he is of familiar and homely friends. As long as you are more concerned for yourself than you are for people you have never seen, you are wrong, and you cannot have even a momentary insight into the simple core of the soul. You may have a symbolic idea of the truth, but this is by no means best.

In the second place, you must be pure in heart, for his heart alone is pure, for whom creatures are as nothing.

In the third place, you must have got rid of all "Not."

They ask, what is burned in hell? Authorities usually

* R. B. Blakney, *Meister Eckhart; a Modern Translation* (New York: Harper & Bros., 1941), pp. 126-27.

reply: "This is what happens to willfulness." But I say it is this "Not" that is burned out in hell. For example: suppose a burning coal is placed on my hand. If I say that the coal burns me, I do it a great injustice. To say precisely what does the burning: it is the "Not." The coal has something in it that my hand has not. Observe!—it is just this "Not" that is burning me—for if my hand had in it what the coal has, and could do what the coal can do, it, too, would blaze with fire, in which case all the fire that ever burned might be spilled on this hand and I should not [feel?] hurt.

Likewise, I should say that because God and all who live in his presence have something like true blessedness in them, such as those who are cut off from God have not, it is only the "Not" [—the need or want of blessing] that punishes souls in hell, rather than any willfulness or other kind of fuel. Truly I say that to the extent "Not" exists in you, you are imperfect, and if you would be perfect you must get rid of it.

Thus my text says: "God sent his only begotten Son into the world"—and by that you must not understand the external world, in which he ate and drank with us, but you should know that it refers to the inner world. As sure as the Father, so single in nature, begets his Son, he begets him in the spirit's inmost recess—and that is the inner world. Here, the core of God is also my core; and the core of my soul, the core of God's, and here, I am independent as God himself is independent. If one could peek into this core [of the soul] even for an instant, he would afterwards think no more of a thousand pounds of beaten red gold than of a counterfeit farthing.

Do all you do, acting from the core of your soul, without a single "Why." I tell you, whenever what you do is done for the sake of the Kingdom of God, or for God's sake, or for eternal blessing, and thus really for ulterior motives, you are wrong. You may pass for a good person, but this is not the best. For, truly, if you imagine that you are going to get more out of God by means of religious offices and devotions, in sweet retreats and solitary orisons, than you might by the fireplace or in the stable, then you might just as well think you could seize God and wrap a mantle around his head and stick him under the table! To seek God by rituals is to get the ritual and lose God in the process, for he hides behind it. On the other hand, to seek God without artifice, is to take him as he is, and so doing, a person "lives by the Son," and is the Life itself.

For if Life were questioned a thousand years and asked: "Why live?" and if there were an answer, it could be no more than this: "I live only to live!" And that is because Life is its own reason for being, springs from its own Source, and goes on and on, without ever asking why—just because it is life. Thus, if you ask a genuine person, that is, one who acts [uncalculatingly] from his heart: "Why are you doing that?"—he will reply in the only possible way: "I do it because I do it!"

Where the creature ends, there God begins to be. God asks only that you get out of his way, in so far as you are creature, and let him be God in you. The least creaturely idea that ever entered your mind is as big as God. Why? Because it will keep God out of you entirely. The moment you get [one of your own] ideas, God fades out and the Godhead too. It is when the idea is gone that God gets in.

God desires urgently that you, the creature, get out of his way—as if his own blessedness depended on it. Ah, beloved people, why don't you let God be God in you? What are you afraid of? You get completely out of his way and he will get out of yours—you give up to him and he will give up to you. When both [God and you] have forsaken self, what remains [between you] is an indivisible union. It is in this unity that the Father begets his Son in the secret spring of your nature. Then the Holy Spirit blooms and out of God there comes a will which belongs to the soul. . . .

B.
From Thomas à Kempis, The Imitation of Christ*

*Chapter XXIV.   Of Self-denial, and the Renunciation
of Animal Desire*

1. WITHOUT a total denial of self, my son, thou canst
not attain the possession of perfect liberty. All self-lovers
and self-seekers are bound in chains of adamant; full of
desires, full of cares, restless wanderers in the narrow circle
of sensual pleasure, perpetually seeking their own luxurious
ease, and not the interests of their self-denying, crucified
Saviour; but often pretending this, and erecting a fabric of
hypocrisy that cannot stand; for all that is not of God, must
perish.

But do thou, my son, keep invariably to this short, but
perfect rule: "Abandon all, and thou shalt possess all: relinquish desire, and thou shalt find rest." Revolve this again
and again in thy mind, and when thou hast transfused it
into thy practice, thou wilt understand all things.

. . .

Chapter XXXIII.   Of the Vanity of Human Learning

1. BE not captivated, my son, by the subtlety and elegance of human compositions; for "the kingdom of God is
not in word, but in power." Attend only to the truths of
my word, which enlighten the understanding, and inflame
the heart; which excite compunction, and pour forth the
balm of true consolation. But read my word, not for the
reputation of critical skill, and controversial wisdom, but
to learn how to mortify thy evil passions; a knowledge of
infinitely more importance, than the solution of all the
abstruse questions that have perplexed men's minds, and
divided their opinions.

2. When, however, thou hast meekly and diligently read
my word, still thou must have recourse to me as the only
principle of divine truth. I am he that teacheth man knowl-

* John Payne, trans., *Thomas à Kempis, The Imitation of
    Christ* (New York: Collins and Brothers, n.d.), pp. 234,
    253-54.

edge, and giveth to the simple that light and understanding which no human instruction can communicate. He who listeneth only to my voice, shall soon become wise, and be renewed in the spirit of truth. But, woe be to them, who, instead of turning to me to learn what is my will, devote their time and labour to the vain theories of human speculation! A day will come, when Christ, the teacher of teachers, the light and Lord of angels, shall appear, and at his omniscient tribunal hear the lessons which conscience has given to all; and then "shall Jerusalem be searched with candles, the hidden things of darkness shall be brought to light;" and the clamorous tongue of reasoning and disputing man shall be silent as the grave!

3. I am he, who exalteth the humble and simple mind, and suddenly imparteth to it such a perception of eternal truth, as it could not acquire by a life of laborious study in the schools of men. I teach not, like men, with the clamour of uncertain words, or the confusion of opposite opinions; with vain learning, or the ostentation of learning yet more vain; or with the strife of formal disputation, in which victory is more contended for than truth; I teach, in still and soft whispers, to relinquish earth, and seek after heaven; to loathe carnal and temporary enjoyments, and sigh for spiritual and eternal; to shun honour, and to bear contempt; to place all hope and dependance upon me, to desire nothing besides me, and above all in heaven and on earth most ardently to love me.

C.
From the Life of St. Teresa*

On the way there, I stopped at the house of this uncle of mine, which, as I have said, was on the road, and he gave me a book called *Third Alphabet*, which treats of the Prayer of Recollection.[1] During this first year I had been

---

* E. A. Peers, ed. and trans., *The Complete Works of Saint Teresa of Jesus* (London and New York: Sheed and Ward, 1957), pp. 23-24, 76, 111, 125-26, 192-93.

[1] The uncle, Don Pedro, lived at Hortigosa, a village on the road to Castellanos. The Discalced Carmelite community

reading good books (I no longer wanted to read any others, for I now realized what harm they had done me) but I did not know how to practise prayer, or how to recollect myself, and so I was delighted with the book and determined to follow that way of prayer with all my might. As by now the Lord had granted me the gift of tears, and I liked reading, I began to spend periods in solitude, to go frequently to confession and to start upon the way of prayer with this book for my guide. For I found no other guide (no confessor, I mean) who understood me, though I sought one for fully twenty years subsequently to the time I am speaking of. This did me great harm, as I had frequent relapses, and might have been completely lost; a guide would at least have helped me to escape when I found myself running the risk of offending God.

In these early days His Majesty began to grant me so many favours that at the end of this entire period of solitude, which lasted for almost nine months, although I was not so free from offending God as the book said one should be, I passed over that, for such great care seemed to me almost impossible. I was particular about not committing mortal sin—and would to God I had always been so! But about venial sins I troubled very little and it was this which brought about my fall. Still, the Lord began to be so gracious to me on this way of prayer that He granted me the favour of leading me to the Prayer of Quiet, and occasionally even to Union, though I did not understand what either of these was, or how highly they were to be valued. Had I understood this I think it would have been a great blessing. It is true that my experience of Union lasted only a short time; I am not sure that it can have been for as long as an *Ave Maria*; but the results of it were so considerable, and lasted for so long that, although at this time I was not twenty years old,[2] I seemed to have trampled the world

---

of St. Joseph, at Ávila, still preserves the copy of Francisco de Osuna's *Third Spiritual Alphabet* here referred to.
[2] [St. Teresa must have been mistaken. She cannot possibly have been less than twenty-three and was probably a little older.]

beneath my feet, and I remember that I used to pity those
who still clung to it, even in things that were lawful. I used
to try to think of Jesus Christ, our Good and our Lord, as
present within me, and it was in this way that I prayed.
If I thought about any incident in His life, I would imagine
it inwardly, though I liked principally to read good books,
and this constituted the whole of my recreation. For God
had not given me talents for reasoning with the understanding or for making good use of the imagination: my
imagination is so poor that, even when I thought about
the Lord's Humanity, or tried to imagine it to myself, as I
was in the habit of doing, I never succeeded. And although, if they persevere, people may attain more quickly
to contemplation by following this method of not labour-
ing with the understanding, it is a very troublesome and
painful process. For if the will has nothing to employ it
and love has no present object with which to busy itself,
the soul finds itself without either support or occupation,
its solitude and aridity cause it great distress and its
thoughts involve it in the severest conflict.
. . .

We may also imitate the saints by striving after solitude
and silence and many other virtues; such things will not
kill these wretched bodies of ours, which want to have
everything organized for their benefit in such a way as to
disorganize the soul and which the devil does his best to
incapacitate when he sees that we are getting fearful about
them. That is quite enough for him: he tries at once to
persuade us that all these habits of devotion will kill us, or
ruin our health; he even makes us afraid that if we weep
we shall go blind. I have experienced this, so I know it—
and I also know that we can desire no better kind of sight
or health than to lose both in so good a cause. As my own
health is so bad, I was always impeded by my fears, and
my devotion was of no value at all until I resolved not to
worry any more about my body or my health; and now I
trouble about them very little. For it pleased God to reveal
to me this device of the devil; and so, whenever the devil
suggested that I should ruin my health, I would reply:
"Even if I die it is of little consequence." "Rest, indeed!"

I would say. "I need no rest; what I need is crosses." And so with other things. I saw clearly that in very many cases, although in fact I have very bad health, it was a temptation either of the devil or of my own weakness; and since I have been less self-regarding and indulgent my health has been very much better. It is of great importance, when we begin to practise prayer, not to let ourselves be frightened by our own thoughts. And you may take my word for this, for I have learned it by experience; this mere narration of my faults might be of use to others if they will take warning by me.

. . .

Chapter XIX

. . . Begins to describe the effects produced in the soul by this degree of prayer. Exhorts souls earnestly not to turn back, even if after receiving this favour they should fall, and not to give up prayer. Describes the harm that will ensue if they do not follow this counsel. This chapter is to be read very carefully and will be of great comfort to the weak and to sinners.

The soul that has experienced this prayer and this union is left with a very great tenderness, of such a kind that it would gladly become consumed, not with pain but in tears of joy. It finds itself bathed in these tears without having been conscious of them or knowing when or how it shed them. But it derives great joy from seeing the vehemence of the fire assuaged by water which makes it burn the more. This sounds like nonsense but none the less it is what happens. Sometimes, when I have reached the end of this prayer, I have been so completely beside myself that I have not known whether it has been a dream or whether the bliss that I have been experiencing has really come to me; and I have only known that it has not been a dream through finding myself bathed in tears, which have been flowing without causing me any distress and with such vehemence and rapidity that it has been as if they had fallen from a cloud in heaven. This would happen to me in the early stages, when the condition soon passed away.

. . .

Let us now return to raptures, and to their most usual characteristics. I can testify that after a rapture my body often seemed as light as if all weight had left it: sometimes this was so noticeable that I could hardly tell when my feet were touching the ground. For, while the rapture lasts, the body often remains as if dead and unable of itself to do anything: it continues all the time as it was when the rapture came upon it—in a sitting position, for example, or with the hands open or shut. The subject rarely loses consciousness: I have sometimes lost it altogether, but only seldom and for but a short time. As a rule the consciousness is disturbed; and, though incapable of action with respect to outward things, the subject can still hear and understand, but only dimly, as though from a long way off. I do not say that he can hear and understand when the rapture is at its highest point—by "highest point" I mean when the faculties are lost through being closely united with God. At that point, in my opinion, he will neither see, nor hear, nor perceive; but, as I said in describing the preceding prayer of union, this complete transformation of the soul in God lasts but a short time, and it is only while it lasts that none of the soul's faculties is able to perceive or know what is taking place. We cannot be meant to understand it while we are on earth—God, in fact, does not wish us to understand it because we have not the capacity for doing so. I have observed this myself.

. . .

It pleased the Lord that I should sometimes see the following vision. I would see beside me, on my left hand, an angel in bodily form—a type of vision which I am not in the habit of seeing, except very rarely. Though I often see representations of angels, my visions of them are of the type which I first mentioned. It pleased the Lord that I should see this angel in the following way. He was not tall, but short, and very beautiful, his face so aflame that he appeared to be one of the highest types of angel who seem to be all afire. They must be those who are called cherubim: they do not tell me their names but I am well aware that there is a great difference between certain angels and others, and between these and others still, of a kind that I could not possibly explain. In his hands I saw a long golden spear and at the end of the iron tip I seemed to see a point of fire. With this he seemed to pierce my heart several times so that it penetrated to my entrails. When he drew it out, I thought he was drawing them out with it and he left me completely afire with a great love for God. The pain was so sharp that it made me utter several moans; and so excessive was the sweetness caused me by this intense pain that one can never wish to lose it, nor will one's soul be content with anything less than God. It is not bodily pain, but spiritual, though the body has a share in it—indeed, a great share. So sweet are the colloquies of love which pass between the soul and God that if anyone thinks I am lying I beseech God, in His goodness, to give him the same experience.

During the days that this continued, I went about as if in a stupor. I had no wish to see or speak with anyone, but only to hug my pain, which caused me greater bliss than any that can come from the whole of creation. I was like this on several occasions, when the Lord was pleased to send me these raptures, and so deep were they that, even when I was with other people, I could not resist them; so, greatly to my distress, they began to be talked about. Since I have had them, I do not feel this pain so much, but only the pain of which I spoke somewhere before—I do not remember in what chapter. The latter is, in many respects, very different from this, and of greater worth. But, when this pain of which I am now speaking begins, the Lord seems to transport the soul and to send it into an ecstasy, so that it cannot possibly suffer or have any pain because it immediately begins to experience fruition. May He be blessed for ever, Who bestows so many favours on one who so ill requites such great benefits.

— Reading No. 3 —

UNORTHODOX SECTS

During the intellectual ferment of the Renaissance much dissatisfaction arose with the beliefs and observances of the Church. Various heretical sects appeared, composed of rebels against orthodoxy and the ecclesiastical system. Notable among them were the Lollards, followers of John Wycliffe in England and Scotland in the fourteenth and fifteenth centuries. They spread also to the Continent and influenced the Hussite movement in Bohemia. Their agitation was not exclusively religious but had political and economic undertones. They resented the worldliness of the Church, its ambitions for political power, and its taxation of starving peasants to support a luxury-loving clergy. They opposed auricular confessions and transubstantiation and taught that temporal possessions ruined the Church, that the requirement of celibacy for the clergy was a cause of unnatural vice, and that all wars were contrary to the New Testament and were nothing but murdering and plundering the poor to win glory for kings. Other beliefs or alleged beliefs of the Lollards are contained in the following reply of Wycliffe to his summons by the Pope to come to Rome in 1384 and in the proceedings against him at London and Constance in 1382 and 1415, respectively.

A.

Reply of Wycliffe to His Summons by the Pope to Come to Rome, 1384 *

I have joy fully to tell to all true men that believe what I hold, and algates to the Pope; for I suppose that if my

* University of Pennsylvania, *Translations and Reprints* (Philadelphia, 1897), vol. II, pp. 13-14.

faith be rightful and given of God, the Pope will gladly confirm it; and if my faith be error, the Pope will wisely amend it.

I suppose over this that the gospel of Christ be heart of the corps of God's law; for I believe that Jesus Christ, that gave in his own person this gospel, is very God and very man, and by this heart passes all other laws.

I suppose over this that the Pope be most obliged to the keeping of the gospel among all men that live here; for the Pope is highest vicar that Christ has here in earth. For moreness of Christ's vicar is not measured by worldly moreness, but by this, that this vicar sues more Christ by virtuous living; for thus teacheth the gospel, that this is the sentence of Christ.

And of this gospel I take as believe, that Christ for time that he walked here, was most poor man of all, both in spirit and in having; for Christ says that he had nought for to rest his head on. And Paul says that he was made needy for our love. And more poor might no man be, neither bodily nor in spirit. And thus Christ put from him all manner of worldly lordship. For the gospel of John telleth that when they would have made Christ king, he fled and hid him from them, for he would none such worldly highness.

And over this I take it as believe, that no man should sue the Pope, nor no saint that now is in heaven, but in as much as he sues Christ. For John and James erred when they coveted worldly highness; and Peter and Paul sinned also when they denied and blasphemed in Christ; but men should not sue them in this, for then they went from Jesus Christ. And this I take as wholesome counsel, that the Pope leave his worldly lordship to worldly lords, as Christ gave them,—and move speedily all his clerks to do so. For thus did Christ, and taught thus his disciples, till the fiend had blinded this world. And it seems to some men that clerks that dwell lastingly in this error against God's law, and flee to sue Christ in this, been open heretics, and their fautors been partners.

And if I err in this sentence, I will meekly be amended, yea, by the death, if it be skilful, for that I hope were good

to me. And if I might travel in mine own person, I would
with good will go to the Pope. But God has needed me to
the contrary, and taught me more obedience to God than
to men. And I suppose of our Pope that he will not be
Antichrist, and reverse Christ in this working, to the contrary of Christ's will; for if he summon against reason, by
him or by any of his, and pursue this unskilful summoning,
he is an open Antichrist. And merciful intent excused not
Peter, that Christ should not clepe him Satan; so blind
intent and wicked counsel excuses not the Pope here; but
if he ask of true priests that they travel more than they
may, he is not excused by reason of God, that he should
not be Antichrist. For our belief teaches us that our blessed
God suffers us not to be tempted more than we may; how
should a man ask such service? And therefore pray we to
God for our Pope Urban the Sixth, that his old holy intent
be not quenched by his enemies. And Christ, that may not
lie, says that the enemies of a man been especially his home
family; and this is sooth of men and fiends.

B.
Propositions of Wycliffe Condemned at London (1382) and at Constance (1415)*

1.[1] That the material substance of bread and the material substance of wine remain in the Sacrament of the
altar.

2. That the accidents of bread do not remain without
a subject (substance) in the said Sacrament.

3. That Christ is not in the Sacrament essentially and
really, in his own corporeal presence.

4. That if a bishop or priest be in mortal sin he does
not ordain, consecrate or baptize.

5. That it is not laid down in the Gospel that Christ
ordained the Mass.

* Henry Bettenson, *Documents of the Christian Church* (New
   York and London: Oxford University Press, 1947), pp.
   246-48.

[1] The propositions are numbered as at Constance.

6. That God ought to obey the devil.

7. That if a man be duly penitent any outward confession is superfluous and useless.

10. That it is contrary to Holy Scripture that ecclesiastics should have possessions.

14. That any deacon or priest may preach the word of God apart from the authority of the Apostolic See or a Catholic bishop.

15. That no one is civil lord, or prelate, or bishop, while he is in mortal sin.

16. That temporal lords can at their will take away temporal goods from the church, when those who hold them are sinful (habitually sinful, not sinning in one act only).

17. That the people can at their own will correct sinful lords.

18. That tithes are mere alms, and that parishioners can withdraw them at their will because of the misdeeds of their curates.

20. That he who gives alms to friars is by that fact excommunicate.

21. That anyone who enters a private religion [i.e. religious house], either of those having property or of mendicants, is rendered more inapt and unfit for the performance of the commands of God.

22. That holy men have sinned in founding private religions.

23. That the religious who live in private religions are not of the Christian religion.

24. That friars are bound to gain their livelihood by the labor of their hands, and not by begging.

[The above are common to the proceedings at London and at Constance. Many other propositions, of which a few are given below, were condemned at Constance. They are more extreme in tone and are probably to be attributed more to the Lollards than to Wycliffe himself.]

28. That the confirmation of young men, the ordination of clerics, the consecration of places are reserved for the Pope and bishops on account of the desire for temporal gain and honor.

30. That the excommunication of the Pope or of any

prelate is not to be feared, because it is the censure of antichrist.

34. That all of the order of mendicants are heretics.

35. That the Roman Church is the synagogue of Satan, and the Pope is not the next and immediate vicar of Christ and the Apostles.

42. That it is fatuous to believe in the indulgences of the Pope and the bishops.

43. That all oaths made to corroborate human contracts and civil business are unlawful.

— Reading No. 4 —

THE JESUITS

No body of men was more important in the Catholic Reformation than the Society of Jesus, founded about 1535 by Ignatius of Loyola. Its members dedicated themselves to the service of the Church with unexampled fervor and devotion. Organized in military fashion, they conceived of themselves as soldiers of Christ committed to the defense of His Church against all schismatic and heretical opposition. They aided the Popes in dominating the Council of Trent. They established the most thorough system of religious education in Europe. It was largely through their educational and missionary efforts that Bavaria, Austria, and Poland were saved or recovered for the ancient faith.

In his efforts to find inner peace, Ignatius of Loyola set down his experiences in a work that came to be called Spiritual Exercises. *In final form it was a book of discipline to enable the individual to control his own will and emotions and thereby gain maximum efficiency in serving the interests of the Church.*

✓ ✓ ✓

A.

From the Spiritual Exercises of Ignatius of Loyola*

GENERAL EXAMINATION OF CONSCIENCE

In order to purify oneself and to confess better.

I presuppose that there are within me three kinds of

* St. Ignatius of Loyola, *The Spiritual Exercises* (New York: Catholic Book Publishing Co., 1948), pp. 38-39, 107-9, 118-20, 160-63, 174-79.

thoughts: one my own, which springs entirely from my own liberty and will; and two others, which come from without, one from the good spirit, and the other from the evil.

OF THOUGHTS

There are two ways of gaining merit from an evil thought which comes from without.

1. For example, a thought comes of committing a mortal sin, which thought I resist promptly, and it remains conquered.

2. When the same evil thought comes to me, and I resist it, and it returns time after time, and I always resist it, until it goes away conquered; and this second way is much more meritorious than the first.

A venial sin is committed when the same thought of sinning mortally comes and one gives ear to it, dwelling a few moments on it, or receiving some slight sensual delectation, or when there is some negligence in rejecting such a thought.

There are two ways of sinning mortally:

1. When a man gives consent to an evil thought with the intention of acting afterwards according to his consent, or with the desire of doing so if he could.

2. When that sin is carried out in action; and this is a more grievous sin for three reasons: first, on account of the longer time; secondly, on account of the greater intensity; thirdly, on account of the greater injury to both persons.

. . .

RULES FOR THE FUTURE

RULES—for ordering oneself for the future in the matter of food.

FIRST RULE. There is less need to abstain from bread, because it is not a food in regard to which the appetite is wont to be so inordinate or the temptation importunate, as with other kinds of food.

SECOND RULE. With regard to drink, abstinence seems more suitable than with regard to eating bread. Therefore, each should consider well what is good for him, that he may allow himself to take it, and what is harmful, that he may reject it.

THIRD RULE. With regard to meats, greater and more entire abstinence must be observed because here the appetite is more ready to exceed and to seek that which delights it. Thus, abstinence in food, in order to avoid excess, may be observed in two ways: the one, by accustoming oneself to eat coarse foods; the other, if one does take delicacies, taking them in small quantities.

FOURTH RULE. Provided health is not injured, the more each can retrench from a sufficient diet, the sooner will he arrive at the mean which he ought to observe in eating and drinking, and that for two reasons: first, because by thus helping and disposing himself he will more often and more abundantly experience interior lights, consolations, and divine inspirations, which will show him the fitting mean; secondly, because if the person sees that such a degree of abstinence does not leave him sufficient strength of body or spirit for the spiritual Exercises, he will easily come to judge what is more suitable for sustaining the body.

FIFTH RULE. While taking his food let him do so as if he saw Christ our Lord eating with His disciples, and consider how He drinks and looks, and speaks. Let him endeavor to imitate Him, in such a way that the mind may principally be occupied with the consideration of Christ our Lord, and less with the sustenance of the body. Thus he may adopt a better order and rule with regard to the manner in which he ought to behave and govern himself.

SIXTH RULE. At another time, while eating, he may take another consideration, reflecting upon the life of the saints, or some pious contemplation, or on some spiritual business he has to do. Thus, having his attention fixed on such matters, he will take less sensible pleasure in his bodily food.

SEVENTH RULE. Above all, let him take care that his whole mind be not intent upon what he is eating, and that in eating he is not carried away by his appetite into eating hurriedly, but let him be master of himself both in his manner of eating and in the quantity he takes.

EIGHTH RULE. In order to overcome excess, it is very useful, after dinner or after supper, or at some other time when one does not feel any desire to eat, to determine with oneself the amount to be taken at the next dinner or supper. In like manner to determine each day the amount which it is fitting to eat, and not by yielding to appetite or temptation, to exceed it; but rather, the better to overcome all inordinate appetite and temptation of the enemy, if he be tempted to eat more, let him eat less.

. . .

METHODS OF PRAYER

PREPARATORY PRAYER. To ask for the grace of God our Lord that I may be able to know in what I have failed with regard to the ten commandments; and likewise to ask for grace and help to amend myself in the future, begging for a perfect understanding of them in order to observe them better, and for the greater glory and praise of His divine Majesty.

On the Ten Commandments

For the first method of prayer it is suitable to consider and to think over the first commandment, how I have kept it, and in what I have been deficient, stopping as a rule in this consideration for the space in which one may recite three times the *Our Father* and three times the *Hail Mary*. If in this time I discover faults of mine, I will ask pardon and forgiveness of them, and say an *Our Father*. And let this be done in the same way in each of all the ten commandments.

It is to be observed that when a man comes to consider a commandment against which he finds he is not wont to sin, it is not necessary to dwell upon it so long; but according as he finds that he more or less offends in any commandment, so he ought to stop a greater or less time in its consideration and examination. Let the same be observed with regard to the deadly sins.

After having gone through in this way all the commandments, accusing myself in regard to them, and asking for grace and help to amend myself in the future, I will end with a colloquy to God our Lord, according to the subject matter.

On Deadly Sins

With regard to the seven deadly sins, after the Addition, let the preparatory prayer be made in the manner already mentioned, the only change being that the matter here is concerned with sins which are to be avoided, whereas before it was concerning commandments which are to be kept. In like manner let the order and rule already laid down be observed, and the colloquy.

In order the better to know the faults committed in the matter of the deadly sins, let their contraries be considered. The better to avoid these sins, let the person resolve and endeavor by means of holy Exercises to acquire and retain the seven virtues contrary to them.

On the Powers of the Soul

With regard to the three powers of the soul, let the same order and rule be observed as in the commandments, making the Addition, preparatory prayer, and colloquy.

On the Five Senses of the Body

With regard to the five senses of the body, the same order will be observed, the subject matter only being changed.

Let him who wishes to imitate Christ our Lord in the use of his senses, recommend himself in the preparatory prayer to His divine Majesty; and after the consideration of each sense let him say a *Hail Mary* or an *Our Father*.

And let him who wishes to imitate our Lady in the use of his senses, commend himself in the preparatory prayer to her, that she may obtain this grace for him from her Son and Lord, and after the consideration of each sense let him say a *Hail Mary*.

. . .

RULES FOR THE DISCERNMENT OF SPIRITS

ELEVENTH RULE. Let him who is in consolation take care to humble and abase himself as much as he can, thinking how little he is worth in time of desolation without such grace or consolation. On the other hand, let him who is in desolation remember that he can do much with the grace which is sufficient to resist all his enemies, if only he strengthens himself in his Creator and Lord.

TWELFTH RULE. The enemy acts like a woman, inasmuch as he is weak perforce, and strong only in desire (to injure). For as it is the nature of a woman, when quarrelling with a man, to lose courage and take to flight when he shows her a bold face; and on the contrary, if the man begins to lose courage and run away, the rage, spite, and ferocity of the woman become very great, and altogether without bounds. In the same manner, it is the nature of our enemy to weaken and lose courage, and in his temptations to take to flight when the person who is exercising himself in spiritual matters shows a bold face to them, acting in a manner diametrically opposed to them; and on the contrary, if the retreatant begins to fear and lose courage in enduring temptation, there is no wild beast so fierce on the face of the earth as is the enemy of human nature in the prosecution of his wicked designs with her ever increasing malice.

THIRTEENTH RULE. He also acts like a false lover, in wishing to be hidden and undiscovered. For as such a false man, speaking with an evil purpose and paying court to the daughter of some good father, or the wife of a good husband, wishes his words and solicitations to be kept secret, and, on the contrary, is much displeased when the daughter discloses to her father, or the wife to her husband, his deceitful words and evil intention, because he easily infers that he will be unable to carry out his design; so in like manner, when the enemy of human nature injects into a holy soul his wiles and blandishments, he wishes and desires that they be received and kept in secret. When they are disclosed to a good confessor, or some other spiritual person who understands his frauds and malice, he is very displeased, because he infers that he will not be able to succeed with the wicked design he has begun, seeing that his manifest frauds are brought to light.

FOURTEENTH RULE. He acts also as a commander does

in order to conquer and despoil the object of his desire. For as a captain and commander of an army, pitching his camp, and reconnoitering the strength and arrangement of a fortress, attacks it on its weakest side; so in like manner the enemy of human nature goes round and explores on all sides all our virtues, theological, cardinal, and moral, and where he finds us weaker, and more necessitous as regards our eternal salvation, there he attacks us, and endeavors to take us by storm.

Rules to the same effect with a fuller discernment of spirits, and more suitable for the Second Week.

FIRST RULE. It belongs to God and His angels to give, in the movements they excite, true gladness and spiritual joy, removing all sadness and perturbation caused by the enemy, whose property it is to fight against such joy and spiritual consolation, suggesting false reasons, subtleties and fallacies without end.

SECOND RULE. It belongs to God our Lord alone to give consolation to the soul without preceding cause; for it is the prerogative of the Creator alone to enter into the soul, to go out of it, and to excite movements in it, drawing it wholly to the love of His Divine Majesty. I say without cause, that is, without any previous perception or knowledge of any object from which such consolation might come to the soul by means of its own acts of understanding and will.

. . .

RULES FOR THINKING WITH THE CHURCH

In order to think truly, as we ought, in the Church Militant, the following rules should be observed.

FIRST RULE. Laying aside all private judgment, we ought to hold our minds prepared and prompt to obey in all things the true Spouse of Christ our Lord, which is our Holy Mother, the hierarchical Church.

SECOND RULE. To praise confession to a priest, and the reception of the Most Holy Sacrament once a year, and much better every month, and much better still every eight days, with requisite and due conditions.

THIRD RULE. To praise the frequent hearing of Mass,

also chants, psalms, and prolonged prayers both in and out of church; likewise the hours ordained at fixed times for the whole divine office, and for prayer of every kind, and all canonical Hours.

FOURTH RULE. To greatly praise Religious Orders, virginity and continency, and matrimony not so much as any of these.

FIFTH RULE. To praise vows of Religion, of obedience, of poverty, of chastity, and of other works of perfection and supererogation. It is to be noticed that since a vow has to do with matters which approach towards evangelical perfection, a vow ought not to be made, in matters which deviate from it, as, for example, to become a trader, or to get married, etc.

SIXTH RULE. To praise the relics of the saints, paying veneration to the relics and praying to the saints; and to praise likewise stations, pilgrimages, indulgences, jubilees, crusades, and candles lighted in churches.

SEVENTH RULE. To praise the enactments of the Church with regard to fasts and abstinences, as those of Lent, Ember Days, Vigils, Fridays and Saturdays; likewise penances, not only interior but also exterior.

EIGHTH RULE. To praise the building and adornment of churches; and also images, and to venerate them according to what they represent.

NINTH RULE. To praise, finally, all the precepts of the Church, preserving a ready mind to seek reasons for defending her, and in no way impugning her.

TENTH RULE. We ought to be more ready to approve and praise the enactments and recommendations, and also the customs of our superiors (than to find fault with them); because although sometimes they may not be or may not have been praiseworthy, still to speak against them, whether in public discourse or before the common people, would give rise to murmurs and scandal, rather than edification. Thus the people would be irritated against their superiors whether temporal or spiritual. Nevertheless, as it does harm to speak ill before the common people of superiors in their absence, so it may be useful to speak of their bad conduct to those who can apply a remedy.

ELEVENTH RULE. To praise theology, positive and scholastic; for as it rather belongs to the positive Doctors, as St. Jerome, St. Augustine, St. Gregory, etc., to move the affections to love and serve God our Lord in all things, so it rather belongs to the scholastics as St. Thomas, St. Bonaventure, and the Master of the Sentences, etc., to define and explain for our times the things necessary to eternal salvation, and to take the lead in impugning and exposing all errors and fallacies. The scholastic Doctors, being more modern, are not only able to avail themselves of the true understanding of Holy Scripture, and of the positive and holy Doctors, but also being themselves illuminated and enlightened by the divine power, they derive assistance from the Councils, Canons, and Constitutions of our holy Mother the Church.

TWELFTH RULE. We ought to guard against making comparisons between ourselves who are now living and the blessed who have passed away. No slight error is committed in this, for example, when it is said: "This man knows more than St. Augustine; he is another St. Francis, or greater than he; he is another St. Paul in virtue and sanctity, etc."

THIRTEENTH RULE. To arrive at the truth in all things, we ought always to be ready to believe that what seems to us white is black, if the hierarchical Church so defines it: believing that between Christ our Lord the Bridegroom and the Church His Bride, there is one and the same Spirit, Who governs and directs us for the salvation of our souls; because our holy Mother the Church is ruled and governed by the same Spirit and our Lord who gave the ten commandments.

FOURTEENTH RULE. Although it is very true that no one can be saved unless he is predestined, and has faith and grace, we must be very careful in our manner of speaking and treating of these subjects.

FIFTEENTH RULE. We ought not habitually to speak much of predestination; but if sometimes mention should be made of it in any way we must so speak that the common people may not fall into any error, and say, as sometimes they do, "If I am predestined to be saved or lost, the question is already determined, and whether I do good or ill there cannot be any other result." Thus, becoming paralyzed they neglect good works conducive to their salvation, and to the spiritual profit of their souls.

SIXTEENTH RULE. In the same way we must take heed lest by speaking much and with great earnestness on faith, without any distinction and explanation, occasion be given to become slothful and negligent in good works, whether before faith is formed by charity or after.

SEVENTEENTH RULE. In like manner we ought not to speak of grace at such length and so vehemently as to give rise to that poisonous teaching which takes away free-will. Accordingly, we may speak of faith and grace, so far as we can with the help of God, for the greater praise of His divine Majesty, but not in such a way, especially in these dangerous times of ours, that works and free-will shall receive any detriment, or come to be accounted for nothing.

EIGHTEENTH RULE. Although it is above all things praiseworthy to serve God our Lord diligently out of pure love, yet we ought greatly to praise the fear of His divine Majesty. Not only is filial fear a pious and most holy thing, but even servile fear, when a man does not attain to anything better and more useful, is of great help towards rising out of mortal sin. After he has risen out of it, he easily attains to filial fear, which is wholly acceptable and pleasing to God our Lord, because it is inseparable from divine love.

— Reading No. 5 —

THE CONCILIAR MOVEMENT

From 1378 to 1417 Latin Christendom was divided into two parts by what is known as the Great Schism. It grew out of a conflict between Pope Boniface VIII and King Philip IV (the Fair) of France. The King's soldiers arrested the Pope, and soon afterward he died. Philip's own candidate was then elected to St. Peter's throne, and the papal capital was transferred to Avignon. In 1378 an effort to restore the papacy to its original capital led to the election of two Popes, one at Avignon and one at Rome. The various countries of Europe lined up in support of the two claimants. Scotland and Ireland, for instance, supported the Avignon Pope, England and Germany the Pope at Rome.

The original purpose of the Conciliar movement was to reunite the Church. Many Europeans believed that a General Council, representing all believers, was the logical agency to accomplish this purpose. As the movement developed, its leaders enlarged their objectives. Many of them wished to make it the supreme authority and to give it the right to dominate and even to depose Popes. They hoped to transform the Church into a democracy, or at least an aristocracy, instead of a monarchy. Others conceived of the General Council as an agency to eliminate abuses and heresies from the Church. These various purposes are illustrated by the following decrees and pronouncements.

A.

The University of Paris and the Great Schism, 1393 *

In 1393 the king of France asked the University of Paris to devise a way of ending the schism. In response to this request, each member of the faculty was asked to propose in writing the way which seemed best to him, and to advance all the possible arguments in its favor. A commission of fifty-four professors, masters, and doctors was then appointed to examine all the proposed ways and means. After mature deliberation this commission proposed three possible ways of ending the schism and drew them up in writing and forwarded them to the king. They discussed at some length the relative advantages and disadvantages of each way. Their letter to the king is a long one. We give only three brief extracts from it, to show the three ways which they proposed.

The first way. Now the first way to end the schism is that both parties should entirely renounce and resign all rights which they may have or claim to have to the papal office. . . .

The second way. But if both cling tenaciously to their rights and refuse to resign, as they have done up to now, we would propose the way of arbitration. That is, that they should together choose worthy and suitable men, or permit such to be chosen in a regular and canonical way, and these shall have the full power and authority to discuss the case and decide it, and if necessary and expedient, and approved by those who according to the canon law have the authority [that is, the cardinals], they may also have the right to proceed to the election of a pope.

The third way. If the rival popes, after being urged in a brotherly and friendly manner, will not accept either of the above ways, there is a third way which we propose as an excellent remedy for this sacrilegious schism. We mean that the matter shall be left to a general council. This general council might be composed, according to canon law, only of prelates, or, since many of them are very illiterate,

---

* O. J. Thatcher and E. H. McNeal, *A Source Book for Medieval History* (New York: Charles Scribner's Sons, 1905), pp. 326-27.

and many of them are bitter partisans of one or the other pope, there might be joined with the prelates an equal number of masters and doctors of theology and law from the faculties of approved universities. Or if this does not seem sufficient to anyone, there might be added besides one or more representatives from cathedral chapters and the chief monastic orders, in order that all decisions might be rendered only after most careful examination and mature deliberation.

B.
An Oath of the Cardinals to Reform the Church. Council of Pisa, 1409 *

In the great councils of Pisa and Constance there were two parties, the one in favor of reforming the church at once and ending the schism afterwards (that is, by electing another pope), and the other in favor of first electing the pope and then carrying out the reform under his direction. The latter party was victorious, but before proceeding to the election, each cardinal was compelled to take an oath that, if elected, he would not dissolve the council until a thorough reform of the church was brought about.

We, each and all, bishops, priests, and deacons of the holy Roman church, congregated in the city of Pisa for the purpose of ending the schism and of restoring the unity of the church, on our word of honor promise God, the holy Roman church, and this holy council now collected here for the aforesaid purpose, that, if any one of us is elected pope, he shall continue the present council and not dissolve it, nor, so far as is in his power, permit it to be dissolved until, through it and with its advice, a proper, reasonable, and sufficient reformation of the universal church in its head and in its members shall have been accomplished.

* *Ibid.,* p. 328.

C.

The Council of Constance
Claims Supreme Authority, 1415 *

This holy synod of Constance, being a general council,
and legally assembled in the Holy Spirit for the praise of
God and for ending the present schism, and for the union
and reformation of the church of God in its head and in its
members, in order more easily, more securely, more completely, and more fully to bring about the union and reformation of the church of God, ordains, declares, and
decrees as follows: And first it declares that this synod,
legally assembled, is a general council, and represents the
catholic church militant and has its authority directly from
Christ; and everybody, of whatever rank or dignity, including also the pope, is bound to obey this council in
those things which pertain to the faith, to the ending of
this schism, and to a general reformation of the church
in its head and members. Likewise it declares that if anyone, of whatever rank, condition, or dignity, including also
the pope, shall refuse to obey the commands, statutes,
ordinances, or orders of this holy council, or of any other
holy council properly assembled, in regard to the ending
of the schism and to the reformation of the church, he shall
be subject to the proper punishment; and unless he re-
pents, he shall be duly punished; and if necessary, recourse
shall be had to other aids of justice.

D.

Pius II, by the Bull "Execrabilis," Condemns Appeals
to a General Council, 1459 †

In the great struggle with the councils the pope had come
out victorious. He had successfully resisted all attempts to
make any important changes in the administration of the
church, or to introduce the reforms which were so loudly
called for. Although the council at Basel had brought the
conciliar idea into disrepute, there were many who still called

* *Ibid.*, pp. 328-29.
† *Ibid.*, p. 332.

for a general council as the only means of securing the reforms which were demanded. Pius II condemned and prohibited all such appeals.

The execrable and hitherto unknown abuse has grown up in our day, that certain persons, imbued with the spirit of rebellion, and not from a desire to secure a better judgment, but to escape the punishment of some offence which they have committed, presume to appeal from the pope to a future council, in spite of the fact that the pope is the vicar of Jesus Christ and to him, in the person of St. Peter, the following was said: "Feed my sheep" [John 21:16] and "Whatsoever thou shalt bind on earth shall be bound in heaven" [Matt. 16:18]. Wishing therefore to expel this pestiferous poison from the church of Christ and to care for the salvation of the flock entrusted to us, and to remove every cause of offence from the fold of our Saviour, with the advice and consent of our brothers, the cardinals of the holy Roman church, and of all the prelates, and of those who have been trained in the canon and civil law, who are at our court, and with our own sure knowledge, we condemn all such appeals and prohibit them as erroneous and detestable.

E.
The Decree "Frequens" Passed by the Council of Constance, 1417 *

A frequent celebration of general councils is an especial means for cultivating the field of the Lord and effecting the destruction of briers, thorns, and thistles, to wit, heresies, errors, and schism, and of bringing forth a most abundant harvest. The neglect to summon these fosters and develops all these evils, as may be plainly seen from a recollection of the past and a consideration of existing conditions. Therefore, by a perpetual edict, we sanction, decree, establish, and ordain that general councils shall be celebrated in the following manner, so that the next one shall follow

* J. H. Robinson, *Readings in European History* (New York: Ginn and Co., 1904), vol. I, pp. 512-13.

the close of this present council at the end of five years. The second shall follow the close of that, at the end of seven years, and councils shall thereafter be celebrated every ten years in such places as the pope shall be required to designate and assign, with the consent and approbation of the council, one month before the close of the council in question, or which, in his absence, the council itself shall designate. Thus, with a certain continuity, a council will always be either in session, or be expected at the expiration of a definite time.

This term may, however, be shortened on account of emergencies, by the supreme pontiff, with the counsel of his brethren, the cardinals of the holy Roman Church, but it may not be hereafter lengthened. The place, moreover, designated for the future council may not be altered without evident necessity. If, however, some complication shall arise, in view of which such a change shall seem necessary, as, for example, a state of siege, a war, a pest, or other obstacles, it shall be permissible for the supreme pontiff, with the consent and subscription of his said brethren, or two thirds of them, to select another appropriate place near the first, which must be within the same country, unless such obstacles, or similar ones, shall exist throughout the whole nation. In that case, the council may be summoned to some appropriate neighboring place, within the bounds of another nation. To this the prelates, and others, who are wont to be summoned to a council, must betake themselves as if that place had been designated from the first. Such change of place, or shortening of the period, the supreme pontiff is required legitimately and solemnly to publish and announce one year before the expiration of the term fixed, that the said persons may be able to come together, for the celebration of the council, within the term specified. . . .

— Reading No. 6 —

THE COUNCIL OF TRENT

The last of the great Church councils before the nineteenth century met in the Imperial city of Trent, just south of Austria, from 1545 to 1563. It was not in continuous session during this time but met in three stages or "assemblies," separated by considerable intervals. Its purpose was not to overthrow Protestantism or to condemn its leaders as heretics, as had been done by the Council of Constance in the case of the Hussite movement, but rather to consolidate what was left of the power and prestige of the Church, to centralize and strengthen its organization, to eliminate glaring abuses, to define obscure doctrines, and to restate its position with respect to doctrines challenged. It issued a large number of canons and decrees and also a Catechism defining and clarifying various doctrines.

✓   ✓   ✓

A.

Examples of the Canons of the Council of Trent*

The formal codification of the doctrines and ordinances of the Roman Catholic Church was one of the most interesting and important results of the great schism of the sixteenth century. In spite of the protests of two Catholic princes at least, Ferdinand I. and the King of France, who advocated some concessions to the demands of their subjects, the Council of Trent adhered to a strictly conservative policy. The method of codification took a positive and a negative form. When a matter had been sufficiently discussed the results were

---

* University of Pennsylvania, *Translations and Reprints* (Philadelphia, 1897), vol. II, pp. 28-29.

ratified in a solemn session in a series of *chapters* setting
forth the accepted view of the church. Following these a
series of *canons* were generally drawn up in which those holding various special opinions were declared accursed. A few
examples of these decrees are given below, illustrating the
central dogmas upon which the sacerdotal organization of the
Roman Catholic Church rests.

Thirteenth Session, Chapter IV.—Since Christ our Redeemer declared that it was truly His body which He
offered up in the form [*sub specie*] of bread, and since the
church has moreover always accepted this belief, this holy
council declares once more that by the consecration of the
bread and the wine the whole substance of the bread is
converted into the substance of the body of Christ our
Lord, and the whole substance of the wine into the substance of his blood, which change is aptly and properly
termed trans-substantiation by the Catholic church.

Thirteenth Session, Canon I.—If any one shall deny that
the body and blood of our Lord Jesus Christ together with
his spirit and divinity, to-wit, Christ all in all, are not truly,
really and materially contained in the holy sacrament of
the Eucharist, and shall assert that the Eucharist is but a
symbol or figure, let him be anathema.

Thirteenth Session, Canon VI.—If any one shall say that
Christ, the only-begotten son of God, is not to be wor-
shipped with the highest form of adoration (*Latriæ*) including external worship, in the holy sacrament of the
Eucharist, or that the Eucharist should not be celebrated
by a special festival, nor borne solemnly about in procession according to the praiseworthy and universal rite and
custom of the holy church, nor held up publicly for the
veneration of the people and that those who adore it are
idolaters, let him be anathema.

Twenty-second Session, Canon I.—If any one shall say
that a real and fitting sacrifice is not offered to God in the
mass, or that nothing is offered except that Christ is given
us to eat, let him be anathema.

Twenty-second Session, Canon II.—If any one shall say
that by the words, "This do in remembrance of me," Christ
did not institute the apostles as priests, or did not ordain

that they themselves and their successors should offer up
His body and blood, let him be anathema.

Twenty-second Session, Canon III.—If any one shall say
that the sacrifice of the mass is only a praiseworthy deed or
act of edification, or that it is simply in commemoration
of the sacrifice on the cross and is not in the nature of
a propitiation; or that it can benefit only him who receives
it and ought not to be offered for the living and the dead,
for sins, punishment, atonement and other necessary things,
let him be anathema.

B.
Canons and Decrees of the Council of Trent*

a. On Scripture and Tradition: Session IV, 8 April 1546

The Holy, Oecumenical and General Synod of Trent
. . . having this aim always before its eyes, that errors may
be removed and the purity of the Gospel be preserved in
the Church, which was before promised through the
prophets in the Holy Scriptures and which our Lord Jesus
Christ the Son of God first published by his own mouth
and then commanded to be preached through his Apostles
to every creature as a source of all saving truth and of
discipline of conduct; and perceiving that this truth and
this discipline are contained in written books and in un-
written traditions, which were received by the Apostles
from the lips of Christ himself, or, by the same Apostles,
at the dictation of the Holy Spirit, and were handed on
and have come down to us; following the example of the
orthodox Fathers, this Synod receives and venerates, with
equal pious affection and reverence, all the books both of
the New and the Old Testaments, since one God is the
author of both, together with the said Traditions, as well
those pertaining to faith as those pertaining to morals, as
having been given either from the lips of Christ or by the
dictation of the Holy Spirit and preserved by unbroken succession in the Catholic Church. . . .

* Henry Bettenson, ed., *Documents of the Christian Church*
   (New York and London: Oxford University Press, 1947),
   pp. 367-70.

b. On Original Sin: Session V, 17 June 1546

1. If anyone does not confess that the first man Adam, when he had transgressed the command of God in Paradise, straightway lost that holiness and righteousness in which he had been established, and through the offense of this disobedience incurred the wrath and indignation of God, and therefore incurred death, which God had before threatened to him, and, with death, captivity under the power of him who thereafter had the power of death, namely the devil, and that the whole of Adam, through the offense of that disobedience, was changed for the worse in respect of body and soul: let him be anathema.

2. If anyone asserts that the disobedience of Adam injured only himself and not his offspring . . . or that . . . only death and the pains of the body were transferred to the whole human race, and not the sin also, which is the death of the soul: let him be anathema [Rom. v. 12].

3. If anyone asserts that the sin of Adam—which in origin is one and which has been transmitted to all mankind by propagation, not through imitation, and is in every man and belongs to him—can be removed either by man's natural powers or by any other remedy than the merit of the one mediator our Lord Jesus Christ. . . .

4. If anyone denies that infants who have just issued from their mother's womb are to be baptized, even if born of baptized parents, or says that they are indeed baptized for the remission of sins but that they are not infected with any original sin from Adam such as would need expiation by the laver of regeneration for the attainment of eternal life; whence it follows that in regard to them the formula of baptism for remission of sins is to be understood not in its true but in a false sense. . . .

c. On Justification: Session VI, January 1547

[The following propositions, among others, were anathematized.]

1. That man can be justified before God by his own works, which are done either in the strength of human

nature or through the teaching of the law, apart from the divine grace through Jesus Christ.

2. That this grace is given through Jesus Christ solely to the end that a man may be able more easily to live justly and to earn eternal life, as if he could, though with great difficulty, do both these through his free will, without grace.

3. That without the prevenient inspiration of the Holy Spirit and his aid a man can believe, hope and love, or can repent, as he should, so that on him the grace of justification may be conferred.

4. That the free will of man, moved and aroused by God, does not co-operate at all by responding to the awakening call of God, so as to dispose and prepare itself for the acquisition of the grace of justification, nor can it refuse that grace, if it so will, but it does nothing at all, like some inanimate thing, and is completely passive.

5. That man's free will has been wholly lost and destroyed after Adam's sin.

6. That it is not in the power of man to make his ways evil, but that evil works as well as good are wrought by God, not just by way of permission but even by his own personal activity; so that the betrayal of Judas is no less his work than the calling of Paul.

7. That all works before justification, for whatever reason they were done, are in truth sins and deserve the hatred of God, or that the more strongly a man strives to dispose himself to receive Grace, the more grievously he sins.

9. That the impious is justified by faith alone—if this means that nothing else is required by way of cooperation in the acquisition of the grace of justification, and that it is in no way necessary for a man to be prepared and disposed by the motion of his own will.

15. That a man reborn and justified is bound by faith to believe that he is assuredly in the number of the predestinate.

23. That a man once justified can no more sin, nor can he lose the grace, and so he that falls into sin was never truly justified; or that it is possible altogether to avoid all sins, even venial sins. . . .

24. That justification once received is not preserved and even increased in the sight of God through good works; but that these same works are only fruits and signs of justification, not causes of its increase.

d. On the Eucharist: Session XIII, October 1551

Chapter 4.   On Transubstantiation

Since Christ our Redeemer said that that which he offered under the appearance of bread was truly his body, it has therefore always been held in the Church of God, and this holy Synod now declares anew, that through consecration of the bread and wine there comes about a conversion of the whole substance of the bread into the substance of the body of Christ our Lord, and of the whole substance of the wine into the substance of his blood. And this conversion is by the Holy Catholic Church conveniently and properly called transubstantiation.

Chapter 5.   On the Worship and Veneration of the Holy Eucharist

And so no place is left for doubting that all Christ's faithful should in their veneration display towards this most Holy Sacrament the full worship of adoration [*latriae cultum*] which is due to the true God, in accordance with the custom always received in the Catholic Church. For it is not the less to be adored because it was instituted by Christ the Lord that it might be taken and eaten.

Canons on the Holy Eucharist

3. On the Eucharist. If anyone denies that in the venerable sacrament of the Eucharist the whole Christ is contained under each species and in each separate part of each species: let him be anathema.

C.
Catechism of the Council of Trent*

*Question II. In what manner Sins are remitted
in the Church*

But this pardon, when first we make a profession of
faith, and are cleansed in holy baptism, is given to us entire
and unqualified, in such wise that no sin, whether original
or actual, of omission or commission, remains to be ex-
piated, no penalty to be paid. But by the grace of baptism,
nevertheless, no one is exempted from all the infirmities of
nature; on the contrary, contending, as we all have to con-
tend, against the motions of concupiscence, which ceaseth
not to incite us to sin, we shall scarcely find one who op-
poses so vigorous a resistance, or who guards his salvation
so vigilantly as to be able to escape from every blow. It
being necessary, therefore, that a power of forgiving sins,
distinct from that of baptism, should exist in the Church,
to her were intrusted the keys of the kingdom of heaven,
by which each one, if penitent, may obtain the remission
of his sins, though he had sinned to the last day of his life.
This truth is vouched by the clearest authority of sacred
Scripture: in St. Matthew, the Lord saith thus to Peter:
*I will give unto thee the keys of the kingdom of heaven:
and whatsoever thou shalt bind upon earth, shall be bound
also in heaven; and whatsoever thou shalt loose on earth,
shall be loosed also in heaven;* and again: *Whatsoever ye
shall bind on earth, shall be bound also in heaven; and
whatsoever ye shall loose upon earth, shall be loosed also in
heaven.* Again, the testimony of St. John assures us that
the Lord, having breathed on the apostles, said: *Receive ye
the Holy Ghost, whose sins ye shall remit, they are remitted
unto them; and whose ye shall retain, they are retained.*[1]
    . . .

* Theodore A. Buckley, trans., *The Catechism of the Council
    of Trent* (London: George Routledge and Co., 1852),
    pp. 111, 231-35, 412-13, 425-26, 540.
[1] Matt. xvi. 19; xviii. 18; John xx. 22, 23.

Question XXXIV. Christ, whole and entire, is present in each Particle of either Species

Nor is it to be omitted, that Christ, whole and entire, is contained not only under either species, but also in each particle of either species. For so writes St. Augustine, *Each receives Christ the Lord, and he is entire in each portion; nor is he diminished for each severally, but gives himself entire in each*. This is, also, an obvious inference from the Evangelists, for we must not suppose that each portion of the bread was consecrated by our Lord, applying to it separately the form of consecration; but that all the bread sufficient to perform the sacred mysteries, and to be distributed to the apostles, was consecrated at the same time, and with the same form. That such was the case, also, in the consecration of the chalice, appears from these words of the Saviour: *Take and divide it among you.*[2] Our expositions hitherto have had for their object to enable pastors to show, that in the sacrament of the Eucharist are contained the true body and blood of Christ.

Question XXXV. After Consecration, none of the Substance of the Matter of this Sacrament remains

The next subject which we proposed to ourselves, and which [the pastors] are to set forth, is, that after consecration the substance of the bread and wine does not remain in the sacrament. This, although well calculated to excite the most profound admiration, is yet a necessary consequence from what has been already proved; for if, after consecration, the body of Christ is really and truly present under the species of bread and wine, not having been there before, it must have become so by change of place, by creation, or by the change of another thing into it. Now that the body of Christ cannot be rendered present by change of place is evident, as it would then cease to be in heaven; for whatever is moved must necessarily cease to occupy the place from which it is moved. Still less can we suppose that the body of Christ is rendered present by creation, an idea which cannot even be conceived in thought.

[2] Luke xxii. 17.

It remains, therefore, that the body of our Lord be contained in the sacrament, because the bread is changed into
it; and therefore it necessarily follows, that none of the
substance of the bread remains.

Question XXXVI. Transubstantiation, as approved by the Councils, has its Foundation in the Scriptures

Hence our fathers and predecessors in the faith, in the
great Council of Lateran, and in that of Florence, confirmed by express decrees the truth of this article. By the
Council of Trent, however, it was still more explicitly defined in these words: *If any one shall say, that in the sacred
and holy sacrament of the Eucharist, the substance of the
bread and wine remains, conjointly with the body and
blood of our Lord Jesus Christ, let him be anathema.* The
doctrine thus defined it was easy to infer from the testimony of Scripture, and, first, from what our Lord himself
said, when instituting this sacrament: *This is my body,*[3] for
the force of the word, *this,* is to point out the entire substance of the thing present; but if the substance of the
bread remained, the words, *This is my body,* would appear
to be by no means said with truth. Again, Christ the Lord
says in John: *The bread which I will give is my flesh for the
life of the world,*[4] thus calling his flesh bread. He added a
little after: *Except ye eat the flesh of the Son of Man, and
drink his blood, ye shall have no life in you;*[5] and again:
My flesh is meat indeed, and my blood is drink indeed.[6]
When, therefore, in terms so clear and perspicuous, he calls
his flesh bread and true food, and his blood true drink, he
appears to have sufficiently declared that none of the substance of the bread and wine remains in the sacrament.

Question XXXIX. The Manner in which this, so wondrous a Conversion, takes place

The exposition of this mystery is most difficult. Pastors
will however endeavour to explain the manner of this admirable conversion to those who have made further prog-

[3] Matt. xxvi. 26.
[4] John vi. 52   [5] vi. 54.   [6] vi. 56.

ress in the knowledge of divine things; for those who are yet rather weak may, it is to be feared, be overwhelmed by the greatness of the subject. This conversion then is such, that the whole substance of the bread is changed, by the divine power, into the whole substance of the body of Christ, and the whole substance of the wine, into the whole substance of the blood of Christ, without any change in our Lord. For Christ is neither generated, nor changed, nor increased, but remains entire in his substance. Declaring this mystery, St. Ambrose says: *Thou seest how operative are the words of Christ. If then so great is the efficacy of the words of the Lord Jesus, as that things should begin to exist that had no existence, the world for instance, with how much greater power can it continue in being things that had existence, and change them into another?* To the same effect other ancient Fathers of most grave authority have written. Thus, St. Augustine says: *We confess that before consecration it is bread and wine, the produce of nature; but after consecration, the body and blood of Christ, which the blessing consecrated. The body,* says Damascene, *is truly united to the Divinity, the body born of the holy Virgin; not that the body assumed itself descends from heaven, but that the bread itself and wine are transmuted into the body and blood of Christ.*

Question XL. This Wondrous Conversion is appropriately called Transubstantiation

This admirable conversion then, as the Sacred Council of Trent has taught, is accurately and appropriately called by the holy Catholic Church *Transubstantiation,* for as natural generation, because in it the form [of existence] is changed, may properly and appropriately be called transformation; so, in like manner, to express the change that takes place in the sacrament of the Eucharist, in which the whole substance of one thing passes into the whole substance of another, the word *Transubstantiation* was rightly and wisely introduced by our predecessors in the faith.

Question XLI. The Manner of Transubstantiation, and the Place in which Christ is in this Sacrament, must not be curiously searched into

But in accordance with the principle so often repeated by the Fathers, the faithful are to be admonished that they do not inquire too curiously into the manner in which this change may be made, for it defies our powers of conception, nor have we any example of it in natural changes, nor in the creation of things itself. The change itself is to be learnt by faith; the manner thereof is not to be made a subject of too curious inquiry. Pastors should also use no less caution in explaining the mysterious manner, in which the body of our Lord is contained whole and entire under the least particle of the bread: such disputations will scarcely ever have to be entered upon; should, however, Christian charity require it, the pastor will recollect previously to fortify the minds of the faithful, by reminding them that *no thing shall be impossible with God.*[7]

. . .

Question XV. Public Functionaries are to be honoured

The same is to be said concerning our conduct towards kings, princes, magistrates, and all others to whose authority we are subject; the honour, respect, and obedience due to whom are explained at large by the apostle to the Romans.[8] He also admonishes us to pray for them;[9] and St. Peter saith: *Submit yourselves to every human creature for God's sake: whether it be to the king as supreme, or unto governors, as unto them that are sent by him.*[10] For if we honour them, that honour is referred to God, for the grade of exalted dignity, because an image of the divine power, commands man's veneration; and in it we also revere the providence of God, who has committed to them the administration of the public office which they hold, and who uses them as the ministers of his power.

[7] Luke i. 37.
[8] Rom. xiii.   [9] 1 Tim. ii. 2.   [10] 1 Pet. ii. 13, sq.

Question XVI. Why we ought to obey even Wicked
Magistrates, and when not

Not that we respect the profligacy or wickedness of men,
should public functionaries be of such a character, but that
we revere the divine authority with which they are invested;
so that—and it may appear matter of great marvel—even
though they be inimical and hostile, nay, implacable, towards us, yet is that not a sufficient reason to exempt us
from evincing great respect towards them. Thus David rendered important services to Saul, when he was the object
of his hatred, as he intimates in these words: *With them
that hated peace, I was peaceable.*[11] But should they issue
a wicked or unjust mandate, they are on no account to be
obeyed; for [such mandate] is not the legitimate exercise
of power, but is an act of injustice and perversity. Having
expounded these matters severally, the pastor will next consider the nature of the reward promised to the observance
of this divine commandment, and the suitableness thereof.

. . .

Question XXI. Men who persecute us are the Ministers and
Agents of God, even though they do so with an Evil Intent

But he, whose benignity is boundless, punishes us not as
enemies, but corrects and chastises us as children. To view
the matter in its proper light, men in such cases are nothing
more than the ministers and agents, as it were, of God; and
although one man may malignantly hate and foster the
worst disposition towards another, yet, without the permission of God, he can in no wise injure him. Influenced by
this reflection, Joseph patiently endured the wicked counsels of his brethren,[12] and David the injuries inflicted on
him by Shimei.[13] To this matter also eminently applies an
argument which St. Chrysostom has seriously and learnedly
handled, that no man is injured but by himself; for let
those who deem themselves injured consider the matter

---

[11] Ps. cxix. 7 (cxx. 7). "I am for peace; but when I speak, they
      [are] for war," in our version.
[12] Gen. xlv. 4, sqq. l. 19, sqq.
[13] 2 Sam. xvi. 10, sqq.

aright, and they will find that in reality they received no
insult or injury from others. For although they may have
experienced actual injury from external causes, yet they
themselves are their own greatest enemies, by wickedly con-
taminating their souls with hatred, desire of revenge, and
envy.

. . .

*Question XXIV. How much Advantage in regard to the
Quiet Passing of our Life we may derive from Meditating
on this Petition*

Finally, let the faithful be admonished to acquiesce im-
plicitly in the simple and absolute will of God; let him who
thinks that he holds a place in society inferior to his dignity, bear his lot with a patient mind: let him not abandon
his own sphere; but *abide in the same calling in which he
was called;*[14] and subject his own judgment to the will of
God, who consults better for our interests, than we ourselves can do by the suggestions of our own desires. If op-
pressed by poverty at home, if by sickness of body, if by
persecutions, if by other troubles and afflictions, we must
be firmly convinced, that none of these things can befall us
without the will of God, which is the supreme reason of all
things; and that therefore we should not suffer ourselves to
be too grievously disturbed by them, but bear them with an
unconquered mind, having always on our lips the words of
the apostles, *The will of the Lord be done,*[15] and those of
holy *Job, The Lord gave, and the Lord hath taken away;
blessed be the name of the Lord.*[16]

[14] 1 Cor. vii. 20; Ephes. iv. 1.   [15] Acts xxi. 14.   [16] Job i. 21.

THE REFORMATION AS A POLITICAL MOVEMENT

Both the Protestant Revolution and the Catholic Reformation had political aspects. The former was to a large extent an expression of the nationalist feeling that had been gathering momentum since the thirteenth century. Because Catholicism was avowedly international in character, it was logical that the Catholic Reformation should have anti-national manifestations. In many cases these took the form of justifications of rebellion against oppression by national monarchs who sought to extend their absolute power over religion as well as over secular affairs. Protestants also had their theories to justify rebellion and even assassination. Both sides issued decrees granting partial or complete toleration, generally for the political purpose of preventing or terminating civil strife and preserving national unity. Typical examples were the Peace of Augsburg and the Edict of Nantes.

✓   ✓   ✓

A.
The Peace of Augsburg, 1555 *

§ 15. In order to bring peace into the holy Empire of the Germanic Nation between the Roman Imperial Majesty and the Electors, Princes, and Estates: let neither his Imperial Majesty nor the Electors, Princes, &c., do any violence or harm to any estate of the Empire on account of

---

* B. J. Kidd, *Documents Illustrative of the Continental Reformation* (Oxford: Clarendon Press, 1911), pp. 363-64.

the Augsburg Confession, but let them enjoy their religious belief, liturgy and ceremonies as well as their estates and other rights and privileges in peace; and complete religious peace shall be obtained only by Christian means of amity, or under threat of the punishment of the imperial ban.

§ 16. Likewise the Estates espousing the Augsburg Confession shall let all the Estates and Princes who cling to the old religion live in absolute peace and in the enjoyment of all their estates, rights and privileges.

§ 17. However, all such as do not belong to the two above-named religions shall not be included in the present peace but be totally excluded from it.

§ 18. And since it has proved to be matter of great dispute what was to happen with the bishoprics, priories, and other ecclesiastical benefices of such Catholic priests as would in course of time abandon the old religion, we have in virtue of the powers of Roman Emperors ordained as follows: Where an archbishop, bishop or prelate or any other priest of our old religion shall abandon the same, his archbishopric, bishopric, prelacy, and other benefices, together with all their income and revenues which he has so far possessed, shall be abandoned by him without any further objection or delay. The chapters and such as are entitled to it by common law or the custom of the place shall elect a person espousing the old religion, who may enter on the possession and enjoyment of all the rights and incomes of the place without any further hindrance and without prejudging any ultimate amicable settlement of religion.

§ 19. Some of the abbeys, monasteries, and other ecclesiastical estates having been confiscated and turned into churches, schools, and charitable institutions, it is herewith ordained that such estates as their original owners had not possessed at the time of the treaty of Passau shall be comprised in the present treaty of peace.

§ 20. The ecclesiastical jurisdiction over the Augsburg Confession, doctrine, appointment of ministers, church usages, orders, and ceremonies hitherto practised (but apart from all the rights of the Electors, Princes and Estates, Colleges and Monasteries, to taxes in money or tithes) shall

from now cease, and the Augsburg Confession shall be left
to the free and untrammelled enjoyment of their religion,
ceremonies, appointment of ministers, as is stated in a sub-
sequent separate article, until the final settlement of religion
shall take place.

§ 23. No Estate shall try to persuade the subjects of
other Estates to abandon their religion nor protect them
against their own magistrates. Such as had from olden times
the rights of patronage are not included in the present
article.

§ 24. In case our subjects, whether belonging to the old
religion or to the Augsburg Confession, should intend leaving their homes, with their wives and children, in order to
settle in another place, they shall neither be hindered in
the sale of their estates after due payment of the local taxes
nor injured in their honour. . . .

B.

Extracts from the Edict of Nantes*

The Edict of Nantes, called the Edict of Henry IV. for the
Pacification of the troubles of his Realm, was given at Nantes
in the month of April, 1598, and published in Parlement
February 15, 1599. It is of great length, containing 92 articles
in the body of the edict, to which are appended 56 special
articles. Out of these a few articles have been selected which
seemed to embody the more important provisions concerning
the settlement of the religious disorders in France.

III. We ordain that the Catholic Apostolic and Roman
religion shall be restored and reëstablished in all places and
localities of this our kingdom and countries subject to our
sway, where the exercise of the same has been interrupted,
in order that it may be peaceably and freely exercised, without any trouble or hindrance. Forbidding very expressly
all persons of whatsoever estate, quality or condition, under
the penalties recited above,[1] from troubling, molesting or

---

* University of Pennsylvania, *Translations and Reprints*, vol.
    III, pp. 30-31.
[1] Of punishment as a breaker of the peace and disturber of the
    public repose.

disturbing ecclesiastics in the celebration of divine service, in the enjoyment or perception of tithes, fruits or revenues of their benefices, and all other rights and dues belonging to them; and that all those who during the troubles have taken possession of churches, houses, goods or revenues belonging to the said ecclesiastics, and who retain and occupy the same, shall surrender to them entire possession and peaceable enjoyment of such rights, liberties and sureties as they had before they were deprived of them. Forbidding thus very expressly to those of the said religion called Reformed [2] to have preaching or perform other exercise of the said religion in churches, houses and habitations of the said ecclesiastics.

VI. And in order to leave no occasion for troubles or differences between our subjects we have permitted and herewith permit those of the said religion called Reformed to live and abide in all the cities and places of this our kingdom and countries of our sway, without being annoyed, molested or compelled to do anything in the matter of religion contrary to their consciences, nor for this reason to be subject to visitation in houses and places where they desire to dwell, upon condition that they comport themselves in other respects according to that which is contained in this our present edict.

VII. It is permitted to all lords, gentlemen and other persons, natives and others as well, making profession of the said religion called Reformed, having high justice or full military tenure[3] [as in Normandy] in our realm or in the countries of our sway, be it as proprietor or in usufruct, in whole or in half, or for a third part, to enjoy in their houses of said high justice or tenure as above mentioned, which they shall be required to name before our bailiffs and seneschals, each one in his jurisdiction, as their principal domiciles, the exercise of the said religion, so long as they there reside; and in their absence their wives, or indeed their family, or any part of the same; and even if the right

---

[2] *"ladite Religion prétendue Réformée."*
[3] *"Fief de Haubert,"* a grade of nobility ranking next below barons.

of high justice or full military tenure be in controversy, nevertheless the exercise of the said religion may be enjoyed, providing the aforesaid persons shall be in actual possession of the said right of high justice, even though our own Procureur Général be a party to the suit. We hereby permit the enjoyment of the said religion in their other houses of high justice or military tenure as aforesaid only when they are there present, and not otherwise: all this equally for themselves, their families and subjects as well as for others who desire to be present.

VIII. In houses of fiefs, where those of the said religion have not the said high justice or military tenure, the exercise of the said religion may be enjoyed for the family alone. It is not however intended, in case there should happen to arrive other persons, up to the number of thirty outside of the family, whether it be upon the occasion of a baptism, visits of friends or otherwise, that this should be cause for investigation: provided also that the said houses shall not be within the cities, towns or villages belonging to Catholic lords other than ourselves, having the right of high justice, in which the said Catholic lords shall have their houses. In which case those of the said religion shall not be able to enjoy said exercise in said towns or villages, unless by permission and leave of said lords high justices, and not otherwise.

IX. We also permit those of the said religion to make and continue the exercise of the same in all villages and places of our dominion where it was established by them and publicly enjoyed several and divers times in the year 1597, up to the end of the month of August, notwithstanding all decrees and judgments to the contrary.

XIII. We very expressly forbid to all those of the said religion the exercise, either in respect to ministry, regulation, discipline or the public instruction of children, and otherwise, in this our kingdom and lands of our dominion, of all that concerns religion, otherwise than in the places permitted and granted by the present Edict.

C.

Charles V's Attempts to Save the Unity of His Empire; Secret Instructions to His Vice Chancellor, 1536 *

OCTOBER, 1536.

In addition to the instructions which you, Messire Mathias Held, our dear and faithful councillor and Vice-Chancellor of the Empire, have already received, drawn up in German, and relating to the business for which we have sent you to Germany we think it essential to confide in you the following secret instructions which you are to impart confidentially to the king, our good brother, and to the most reverend Cardinal of *Trante*[1] without, however, allowing the matter to reach the ears of any one else.

First you shall inform my lord, our brother, concerning what you saw and heard of public matters up to the time of your departure, and of the existing relations with the Pope, the Venetians, and other powers of Italy, as well as with the kings of France and of England. Of these matters we shall say no more here since we do not wish to lengthen this instruction unduly, and are, moreover, expecting more exact information of the status of affairs. You will also speak of the conditions in Flanders, and of various other matters which can be more advantageously communicated by you than written.

The information which you might otherwise convey to our brother, as to the policy which we desire and are in a position to adopt, cannot well be formulated, without learning first what action the said King of France will take in regard to peace and the conditions which we have offered in the case of Milan. These you have seen, and of them you have a copy. We must, moreover, learn what farther violence the said king will resort to. Inform our brother of the measures we have taken to learn as soon as possible if matters can be arranged. He must, moreover, be made aware of the measures which the Pope, the Venetians and the other powers will take should the king of France obsti-

* *Ibid.*, vol. II, pp. 24-28.
[1] The editors are not certain what place is meant here.

nately continue the war. It is further very essential to learn
the aim and intentions of the electors, princes and estates
of the Empire in respect to the matters with which you are
commissioned, not only as regards the question of the faith,
but concerning the sympathy and assistance which we may
expect and hope from them. You must exercise the greatest
diligence and prudence in this matter and inform us of the
disposition which you find.

In view of the ill-will which the king of France has always shown, and the frequent negotiations for peace which
have come to naught, we are inclined to doubt whether any
results will be reached in the present case, hence it is especially important that you should make every effort to learn
what can be done to gain the favor and assistance of Germany in case of the continuance of the war.

It must always be kept in mind that the division in Germany is at bottom entirely due to the controversy in regard
to our holy religion. This prevents Germany from being
united as it should be in obedience to us and the holy Empire. This encourages the king of France, moreover, to per-
sist in the war, and furnishes him an obvious excuse for
impeding in a most unwarrantable fashion the meeting of
the council. The confusion may even become worse in view
of the said king's favorable attitude towards the Turks,
should no means be found to restore peace. This point
must be emphasized in Germany and some agreement ought
to be reached as to the measures which should be adopted
in case the Pope, through the influence of the said king of
France or through fear on the part of the Holy Father of
losing his authority in the kingdom of France,[2] should
refuse to consent to the calling of the council, on the
ground of the war between us and the king of France or
for other reasons. To say the truth it would seem in spite
of the evil deeds of the king of France, which are notorious and proven beyond the chance of doubt, that the
Holy Father does not care to take any measures against
the king, but that he will in a word remain neutral until

---

[2] Henry VIII. had but just thrown off the allegiance to the
    Popes.

he discovers which is in the wrong, as if the king of France had committed no offences up to the present and our actions belonged in the same category. He would seem to excuse himself and escape responsibility on the ground that he ought to arbitrate between us as a father, and that, especially, he fears the loss of his authority in France. He may in this way be simply disguising the partiality which he constantly showed towards France before he became Pope.

It is, however, none the less true that in spite of the anxiety caused by the attitude of the Holy Father and the obstinacy of the king of France, we do not wish to use our power in any way against the apostolic authority and dignity or do anything prejudicial, directly or indirectly, to the essentials of our religion or the holy Catholic institutions. But we see clearly that should the Pope continue to maintain his attitude of indifference or dissimulation and not frankly consent to a council, it is all the more necessary that some means should be devised as soon as possible to prevent an increase of confusion in Germany, which will cause the destruction both of religion and the imperial authority. Owing to this disorder we are prevented from doing anything for Christianity itself or towards the defence against the Turks, whom the king of France is constantly encouraging. Our power is thus paralyzed to an extent which manifestly jeopardizes our realms and estates and those of our brother.

For these reasons, while maintaining the great secrecy which the affair demands, you should confer very particularly with my lord our brother, as to whether there be any way of celebrating the council, should Germany consent, even if the said Pope and king of France should not agree to it, and as to how this may be done and with what certainty. This would seem to be a plan based upon perfect right and reason, and all the more because the Holy Father has already promised a council and pledged himself expressly for the king of France.[3] The principal need of a

[3] The editors cannot be sure that this is the proper rendering of the obscure passage in the original.

council is moreover for the German nation. The king of
Portugal will consent to and support the plan as will probably the king of Poland, and the most of the powers of
Italy. As for England, since it is utterly schismatic, the
Pope and the king of France cannot validly allege the fact
that that country was not included, against the legitimacy
of the council.

Should the resort to a council in Germany, with the approbation of all or the greater part of that nation, prove
impracticable, it should be determined whether there is not
some other expedient, for example, to assure those who
have fallen from the faith that no further coercion will be
used if they will but sincerely conform with the other
members of Germany in maintaining peace at home and in
coöperating with our said brother and ourselves, or might
not the treaty of Nuremberg be modified or such a new
one drawn up as the change of times and altered circumstances might dictate. Or may it not be advisable to call
a national assembly in Germany and adjust or neglect (*dis-
simuler*[4]) such matters as may not be essential to our holy
religion. Or let some other expedient be devised so that the
imperial, Roman authority be not sacrificed, as well as our
said brother and ourselves, even should it not supply a
remedy in the matter of religion. For we can but wait until
God grants such remedy as He shall judge fitting to His
holy service, since He knows the regret with which our
said brother and we behold the sad state of affairs, and that
our aim and desire is to serve Him and apply ourselves to
cure the existing evils so soon as any means shall offer
themselves.

We are thus placed in a difficult and critical position, for
we cannot have peace if our enemy does not consent, for,
as it is well known, he is as obstinate as he is powerful,
and regards neither God nor good faith, placing his chief
hope in the division of Germany and the difference in religious matters which exists there, as well as in the approach
of the Turk, whom, as it is reported, he spares no efforts

[4] How much the Emperor meant frankly to concede cannot be
inferred from this vague language.

to encourage. In view of this it behooves our brother to turn his attention to this matter, since everything is at stake, and to find some way of settling his difficulties in Hungary and any other complications in which he may be involved. For it would be quite impossible for us to lend him any assistance, being, as we are, far in arrears for the outlays we have been forced to make in the past. Our kingdoms and countries are so surcharged with burdens that we do not know where we are to look for the absolutely necessary means of continuing this war. This is one of the chief motives which induces us to return to our Spanish kingdoms in order to take council there as to what may be done.

Say, moreover, to our said brother that the reports which are being continually brought to us of the conduct of his court and of the government of certain of his officers and councillors are of a character which makes them incredible to us. We are confident that in view of what he has promised in several letters in his own hand, and by the most reverend Cardinal of *Trante* and others of his and our ministers, he will remedy this state of affairs, which is but right and for his own good and profit and the advantage of his subjects (*des siennes*) whom we look upon as our own. In this way the unfortunate rumors may be counteracted. Nor in this matter would we in any way force or importune him to adopt any measures which his own great discretion does not recognize as essential. But the love more than fraternal which we entertain towards him leads us, in view of what you have known all along, and the reports which continue to reach us, as well as of our urgent wish to remedy the evil, to request him once more with all the love of which we are capable to attend to this matter which is of the utmost weight. . . .

D.
The Abdication of Charles V. Speech at Brussels.*

Although Philibert has fully explained to you, my friends, the causes which have determined me to surrender these

* *Ibid.*, vol. III, pp. 2-4.

states and leave them to my son Don Philip, in order that he may possess and rule them, yet I wish to say certain things with my own mouth. You will remember that upon the 5th of February of this year there had elapsed forty years since my grandfather the emperor Maximilian, in the same place and at the same hour declared my majority at the age of fifteen, withdrew me from the guardianship under which I had remained up to that time and made me master of myself. The following year, which was my sixteenth, king Ferdinand died, my mother's father and my grandfather, in the kingdom over which I then commenced to reign, because my beloved mother, who has but lately died, was left, after the death of my father, with disordered judgment and never sufficiently recovered her health to become mistress of herself.

At that time I went to Spain, by way of the sea. Soon came the death of my grandfather Maximilian in my 19th year and although I was still young they conferred upon me in his stead the imperial dignity. I had no inordinate ambition to rule a multitude of kingdoms, but merely sought to secure the welfare of Germany, to provide for the defence of Flanders, to consecrate my forces to the safety of Christianity against the Turk and to labor for the extension of the Christian religion. But although such zeal was mine, I was unable to show so much of it as I might have wished, on account of the troubles raised by the heresies of Luther and the other innovators of Germany, and on account of serious war into which the hostility and envy of neighboring princes had driven me, and from which I have safely emerged, thanks to the favor of God.

This is the fourth time that I go to Spain, there to bury myself. I wish to say to you that nothing I have ever experienced has given me so much pain or rested so heavily upon my soul as that which I experience in parting from you to-day, without leaving behind me that peace and quiet which I so much desired. My sister Mary who in my absence has governed you so wisely and defended you so well, has explained to you, in the last assembly, the reasons for my determination. I am no longer able to attend to my affairs without great bodily fatigue and consequent detriment to the affairs of the state. The cares which so great a responsibility involves; the extreme dejection which it causes; my health already ruined; all these leave me no longer the strength sufficient for governing the states which God has confided to me. The little strength that remains to me is rapidly disappearing. So I should long ago have put down the burden, if my son's immaturity and my mother's incapacity had not forced both my spirit and my body to sustain its weight until this hour.

The last time that I went to Germany I had determined to do what you see me do to-day, but I could not bring myself to do it when I saw the wretched condition of the Christian state, a prey to such a multitude of disturbances, of innovations, of singular opinions as to faith, of worse than civil wars, and fallen finally into so many lamentable disorders. I was turned from my purpose because my ills were not yet so great, and I hoped to make an end of all these things and restore the peace. In order that I might not be wanting in my duty I risked my strength, my goods, my repose and my life for the safety of Christianity and the defence of my subjects. From this struggle I emerged with a portion of the things I desired. But the king of France and certain Germans, failing to preserve the peace and amity they had sworn, marched against me and were upon the point of seizing my person. The king of France took the city of Metz, and I, in the dead of winter exposed to intense cold, in the midst of snow and blood, advanced with a powerful army raised at my own expense to retake the city and restore the Empire. The Germans saw that I had not yet laid aside the imperial crown and had no disposition to allow its majesty to be diminished.

I have carried out what God has permitted, since the outcome of our efforts depends upon the will of God. We human beings act according to our powers, our strength, our spirit, and God awards the victory and permits defeat. I have ever done as I was able, and God has aided me. I return to Him boundless thanks for having succored me in my greatest trials and in all my dangers.

To-day I feel so exhausted that I should not be of any

aid to you, as you see yourselves. In my present state of dejection and weakness, I should have to render a great and serious account to God and man, if I did not lay aside authority, as I have resolved to do, since my son, king Philip, is of an age sufficiently advanced to be able to govern you, and he will be, I hope, a good prince to all my beloved subjects.

I am determined then to retire to Spain, to yield to my son Philip the possession of all my states, and to my brother, the king of the Romans, the Empire. I particularly commend to you my son, and I ask of you in remembrance of me, that you extend to him the love which you have always borne towards me; moreover I ask you to preserve among yourselves the same affection and harmony. Be obedient towards justice, zealous in the observance of the laws, preserve respect for all that merits it, and do not refuse to grant to authority the support of which it stands in need.

Above all, beware of infection from the sects of neighboring lands. Extirpate at once the germs, if they appear in your midst, for fear lest they may spread abroad and utterly overthrow your state, and lest you may fall into the direst calamities. As to the manner in which I have governed you I confess that I have been more than once deceived, led astray by the inexperience of youth, by the hasty conclusions of young manhood, or by some other fault of human weakness. Nevertheless I make bold to assert, that never of my knowledge or by my will has wrong or violence been done to any of my subjects. If then any can complain of having suffered such, I aver that it is unknown to me and against my will: I declare before all the world that I regret it from the bottom of my heart, and I beseech all present, and those who are not here as well, to wish me well and to pardon me.

E.
Philip II of Spain*

We have several descriptions of Philip II, the most important and impartial of which are those of the Venetian ambassadors. The king's affability, industry, religion, and frail constitution are mentioned by all. In his earlier years, however, he exhibited a Castilian haughtiness which he successfully overcame later.

The Catholic king was born in Spain, in the month of May, 1527, and spent a great part of his youth in that kingdom. Here, in accordance with the customs of the country and the wishes of his father and mother,—who belonged to the house of Portugal,—he was treated with all the deference and respect which seemed due to the son of the greatest emperor whom Christendom had ever had, and to the heir to such a number of realms and to such grandeur. As a result of this education, when the king left Spain for the first time and visited Flanders, passing on his way through Italy and Germany, he everywhere made an impression of haughtiness and severity, so that the Italians liked him but little, the Flemings were quite disgusted with him, and the Germans hated him heartily. But when he had been warned by the cardinal of Trent and Queen Mary [of Hungary, his aunt], and above all by his father, that this haughtiness was not in place in a prince destined to rule over a number of nations so different in manners and sentiment, he altered his manner so completely that on his second journey, when he went to England, he everywhere exhibited such distinguished mildness and affability that no prince has ever surpassed him in these traits. Although his actions display that royal dignity and gravity which are natural and habitual to him, he is none the less agreeable for this; on the contrary, his courtesy toward all seems only the more striking. His pleasing figure, his manly air, and his suavity of speech and manner serve to enhance

* J. H. Robinson, *Readings in European History* (Boston: Ginn & Co., 1906), Vol. II, pp. 168-69.

the pleasing effect. He is slight in stature, but so well built, so admirably proportioned, and dressed with such taste and discernment that one could hardly imagine anything more perfect. . . .

Although the king resembles his father in his face and speech, in his attention to his religious duties, and in his habitual kindness and good faith, he nevertheless differs from him in several of those respects in which the greatness of rulers, after all, lies. The emperor was addicted to war, which he well understood; the king knows but little of it and has no love for it. The emperor undertook great enterprises with enthusiasm; his son avoids them. The father was fond of planning great things and would in the end realize his wishes by his skill; his son, on the contrary, pays less attention to augmenting his own greatness than to hindering that of others. The emperor never allowed himself to be influenced by threats or fear, while the king has lost some of his dominions owing to unreasonable apprehensions. The father was guided in all matters by his own opinion; the son follows the opinions of others.

In the king's eyes no nation is superior to the Spaniards. It is among them that he lives, it is they that he consults, and it is they that direct his policy; in all this he is acting quite contrary to the habit of his father. He thinks little of the Italians and Flemish and still less of the Germans. Although he may employ the chief men of all the countries over which he rules, he admits none of them to his secret counsels, but utilizes their services only in military affairs, and then perhaps not so much because he really esteems them, as in the hope that he will in this way prevent his enemies from making use of them.

— Reading No. 8 —

RESULTS OF THE REFORMATION

Both phases of the Reformation, the Catholic as well as the Protestant, bore fruit in a resurgence of superstition and an increase in intolerance and persecution. Most of the superstitions, of course, were of medieval origin, but the hatreds engendered by sectarian conflict gave them a virulence they had not hitherto possessed. The same can be said of bigotry and persecution. Systematic persecution of heretics had occurred in the thirteenth century, and it had been justified by leading doctors of theology. The Inquisition also was of medieval origin. But such instruments of persecution were not generally used with anything like the malignance they attained during the period of the Reformation. The great exception, of course, was the Spanish Inquisition. During the eighteen years (1480-1498) that this institution was under the direction of Torquemada, it is alleged to have burned 2,000 victims. But the purpose of these executions was largely political, since the Spanish Inquisition was established primarily to eliminate the Moors and thereby to facilitate the unification of the country. Yet another new element characterized the persecutions of the Reformation period. This was the exile, imprisonment, torture, and execution of men of learning. Both Catholics and Protestants numbered among their victims some of the most distinguished scientists and philosophers of their time.

A.
Medieval Superstitions *

*Woman Is Punished for Scattering the Host
upon Her Vegetables*

On a certain island there was a certain possessed girl,
not a nun, whom I myself saw there. When the devil was
asked by a priest why he had so long and so cruelly tortured Hartdyfa de Cogheme, he replied through the mouth
of the girl. "Why? She has most certainly deserved it. She
scattered the Most High upon her vegetables."

Since he did not at all understand the saying, and the
devil was unwilling to explain, the priest went to the woman
and told her what the devil had said about her, advising her
not to deny it, if she understood the saying. She immediately confessed her guilt, saying, "I well understand the
saying, although I have never told any man of it. When I
was a young girl and had a garden to cultivate, I received
a wandering woman as a guest one night. When I told her
of my losses in my garden, saying that all the vegetables
were being devoured by caterpillars, she replied, 'I will tell
you a good remedy. Receive the body of the Lord, break
it in pieces, and scatter it upon your vegetables. And the
caterpillars will disappear at once.' I, wretched one! who
cared more for my garden than for the sacrament, when I
received the body of our Lord at Easter, took it out of my
mouth and did with it as I had been taught. What I had
intended as a remedy for my vegetables, became a source
of torment to me, as the devil is my witness."

NOVICE: "That woman was more cruel than the attend-
ants of Pilate, who spared Jesus after His death, and did
break up His bones."

MONK: "Therefore, up to the present day she atones for
that heinous sin and suffers unheard of tortures. Let those
who employ the divine sacrament for temporal gain, or—
what is more execrable—for evil-doing, give heed to this

* University of Pennsylvania, *Translations and Reprints*, vol.
   II, pp. 19-20.

punishment. Also if vermin neglect to do reverence to this sacrament, they sometimes suffer punishment."

Bees Construct a Church for the Host

For I have heard that a certain rustic, wishing to become wealthy and having many hives of bees, asked certain evil men how he could get rich and increase the number of his bees. He was told by someone that if he retained the sacred communion on Easter and placed it in some one of his hives, he would entice away all of his neighbor's bees, which leaving their own hives, would come to the place where the body of our Lord was and there would make honey. He did this.

Then all the bees came to the hive where the body of Christ was, and just as if they had felt compassion for the irreverence done to it, by their labor they began to construct a little church and to erect foundations, and bases, and columns, and an altar with like labor. And with the greatest reverence they placed the body of our Lord upon the altar. And within that little bee-hive they formed that little church with wonderful and the most beautiful workmanship. The bees of the vicinity leaving their hives came to that one; and over that work they sang in their own manner certain wonderful melodies like hymns.

The rustic hearing this, wondered. But waiting until the fitting time for collecting the honey, he found nothing in his hives in which the bees had been accustomed to make honey. And finding himself impoverished through the means by which he had expected to be enriched, he went to that one where he had placed the host, where he saw the bees had come together. But when he approached, just as if they had wanted to vindicate the insult to our Saviour, the bees rushed upon the rustic and stung him so severely that he escaped with difficulty, and in great agony. Going to the priest he related all that he had done and what the bees had done.

The priest, by the advice of his bishop, collected his parishioners and made a procession to the place. Then the bees leaving the hive, rose in the air, making sweet melody.

Raising the hive they found inside the noble structure of that little church, and the body of our Lord placed upon the altar. Then returning thanks they bore to their own church that little church of the bees constructed with such skill and elegance, and placed it on the altar.

By this deed those, who do not reverence, but offer insult instead to the sacred body of Christ or the sacred place where it is, ought to be put to great confusion.

B.
The Witch-Persecution at Bamberg*

In 1628 there was tried for witchcraft at the episcopal city of Bamberg, in Germany, the Burgomaster Johannes Junius. The minutes of the trial, which is in all respects a fair specimen of witch-trials in general, are still to be seen at Bamberg. Translated from German into English, the greater part runs as follows:

. . . On Wednesday, June 28, 1628, was examined without torture, Johannes Junius, Burgomaster at Bamberg, on the charge of witchcraft: how and in what fashion he had fallen into that vice. Is fifty-five years old, and was born at Niederwaysich in the Wetterau. Says he is wholly innocent, knows nothing of the crime, has never in his life renounced God; says that he is wronged before God and the world, would like to hear of a single human being who has seen him at such gatherings [as the witch-sabbaths].

Confrontation of Dr. Georg Adam Haan. Tells him to his face he will stake his life on it [er wolle darauf leben und sterben], that he saw him, Junius, a year and a half ago at a witch-gathering in the electoral council-room, where they ate and drank. Accused denies the same wholly.

Confronted with Hopffens Elsse. Tells him likewise that he was on Haupts-moor at a witch-dance; but first the holy wafer was desecrated. Junius denies. Hereupon he was told that his accomplices had confessed against him and was given time for thought.

On Friday, June 30, 1628, the aforesaid Junius was

* Ibid., vol. III, pp. 23-27.

again without torture exhorted to confess, but again confessed nothing, whereupon, . . . since he would confess nothing, he was put to the torture, and first the

Thumb-screws were applied. Says he has never denied God his Savior nor suffered himself to be otherwise baptized; will again stake his life on it; feels no pain in the thumb-screws.

Leg-screws. Will confess absolutely nothing; knows nothing about it. He has never renounced God; will never do such a thing; has never been guilty of this vice; feels likewise no pain.

Is stripped and examined; on his right side is found a bluish mark, like a clover leaf, is thrice pricked therein, but feels no pain and no blood flows out.

Strappado. He has never renounced God; God will not forsake him; if he were such a wretch he would not let himself be so tortured; God must show some token of his innocence. He knows nothing about witchcraft. . . .

On July 5, the above named Junius is without torture, but with urgent persuasions, exhorted to confess, and at last begins and confesses:

When in the year 1624 his law-suit at Rothweil cost him some six hundred florins, he had gone out, in the month of August, into his orchard at Friedrichsbronnen; and, as he sat there in thought, there had come to him a woman like a grass-maid, who had asked him why he sat there so sorrowful; he had answered that he was not despondent, but she had led him by seductive speeches to yield him to her will. . . . And thereafter this wench had changed into the form of a goat, which bleated and said, "Now you see with whom you have had to do. You must be mine or I will forthwith break your neck." Thereupon he had been frightened, and trembled all over for fear. Then the transformed spirit had seized him by the throat and demanded that he should renounce God Almighty, whereupon Junius said, "God forbid," and thereupon the spirit vanished through the power of these words. Yet it came straightway back, brought more people with it, and persistently demanded of him that he renounce God in Heaven and all the heavenly host, by which terrible threatening he was obliged to speak this formula: "I renounce God in Heaven and his host, and will henceforward recognize the Devil as my God."

After the renunciation he was so far persuaded by those present and by the evil spirit that he suffered himself to be otherwise baptized [1] in the evil spirit's name. The Morhauptin had given him a ducat as dower-gold, which afterward became only a potsherd.

He was then named Krix. His paramour he had to call Vixen. Those present had congratulated him in Beelzebub's name and said that they were now all alike. At this baptism of his there were among others the aforesaid Christiana Morhauptin, the young Geiserlin, Paul Glaser, [and others]. After this they had dispersed.

At this time his paramour had promised to provide him with money, and from time to time to take him to other witch-gatherings.

. . . Whenever he wished to ride forth [to the witch-sabbath] a black dog had come before his bed, which said to him that he must go with him, whereupon he had seated himself upon the dog and the dog had raised himself in the Devil's name and so had fared forth.

About two years ago he was taken to the electoral council-room, at the left hand as one goes in. Above at a table were seated the Chancellor, the Burgomaster Neydekher, Dr. Georg Haan, [and many others]. Since his eyes were not good, he could not recognize more persons.

More time for consideration was now given him. On July 7, the aforesaid Junius was again examined, to know what further had occurred to him to confess. He confesses that about two months ago, on the day after an execution was held, he was at a witch-dance at the Black Cross, where Beelzebub had shown himself to them all and said expressly to their faces that they must all be burned together on this spot, and had ridiculed and taunted those present. . . .

[1] "Otherwise baptized" is the usual phrase for the rite, a parody of baptism, by which the Devil was believed to initiate his followers.

Of crimes. His paramour had immediately after his se-
duction demanded that he should make away with his
youngest son Hans Georg, and had given him for this purpose a gray powder; this, however, being too hard for him,
he had made away with his horse, a brown, instead.

His paramour had also often spurred him on to kill his
daughter, . . . and because he would not do this he had
been maltreated with blows by the evil spirit.

Once at the suggestion of his paramour he had taken the
holy wafer out of his mouth and given it to her. . . .

A week before his arrest as he was going to St. Martin's
church the Devil met him on the way, in the form of a
goat, and told him that he would soon be imprisoned, but
that he should not trouble himself—he would soon set him
free. Besides this, by his soul's salvation, he knew nothing
further; but what he had spoken was the pure truth; on
that he would stake his life. On August 6, 1628, there was
read to the aforesaid Junius this his confession, which he
then wholly ratified and confirmed, and was willing to
stake his life upon it. And afterward he voluntarily confirmed the same before the court.

[So ended the trial of Junius, and he was accordingly burned
at the stake. But it so happens that there is also preserved in
Bamberg a letter, in quivering hand, secretly written by him
to his daughter while in the midst of his trial (July 24,
1628):]

Many hundred thousand good-nights, dearly beloved
daughter Veronica. Innocent have I come into prison, innocent have I been tortured, innocent must I die. For
whoever comes into the witch prison must become a witch
or be tortured until he invents something out of his head
and—God pity him—bethinks him of something. I will tell
you how it has gone with me. When I was the first time
put to the torture, Dr. Braun, Dr. Kötzendörffer, and two
strange doctors were there. Then Dr. Braun asks me, "Kins-
man, how come you here?" I answer, "Through falsehood,
through misfortune." "Hear, you," he says, "you are a
witch; will you confess it voluntarily? If not, we'll bring in

witnesses and the executioner for you." I said "I am no
witch, I have a pure conscience in the matter; if there are
a thousand witnesses, I am not anxious, but I'll gladly hear
the witnesses." Now the chancellor's son was set before me
. . . and afterward Hoppfen Elss. She had seen me dance
on Haupts-moor. . . . I answered: "I have never renounced God, and will never do it—God graciously keep
me from it. I'll rather bear whatever I must." And then
came also—God in highest Heaven have mercy—the executioner, and put the thumb-screws on me, both hands
bound together, so that the blood ran out at the nails and
everywhere, so that for four weeks I could not use my
hands, as you can see from the writing. . . . Thereafter
they first stripped me, bound my hands behind me, and
drew me up in the torture.[2] Then I thought heaven and
earth were at an end; eight times did they draw me up and
let me fall again, so that I suffered terrible agony. . . .

And this happened on Friday, June 30, and with God's
help I had to bear the torture. . . . When at last the executioner led me back into the prison, he said to me: "Sir,
I beg you, for God's sake confess something, whether it be
true or not. Invent something, for you cannot endure the
torture which you will be put to; and, even if you bear it
all, yet you will not escape, not even if you were an earl,
but one torture will follow after another until you say you
are a witch. Not before that," he said, "will they let you
go, as you may see by all their trials, for one is just like
another." . . .

And so I begged, since I was in wretched plight, to be
given one day for thought and a priest. The priest was
refused me, but the time for thought was given. Now, my
dear child, see in what hazard I stood and still stand. I
must say that I am a witch, though I am not,—must now

---

[2] This torture of the strappado, which was that in most common
    use by the courts, consisted of a rope, attached to the
    hands of the prisoner (bound behind his back) and car-
    ried over a pulley at the ceiling. By this he was drawn up
    and left hanging. To increase the pain, weights were at-
    tached to his feet or he was suddenly jerked up and let
    drop.

renounce God, though I have never done it before. Day
and night I was deeply troubled, but at last there came to
me a new idea. I would not be anxious, but, since I had
been given no priest with whom I could take counsel, I
would myself think of something and say it. It were surely
better that I just say it with mouth and words, even though
I had not really done it; and afterwards I would confess
it to the priest, and let those answer for it who compel me
to do it. . . .

C.
The Duty of Persecution for Witchcraft*

Jean Bodin, jurist and statesman, was not only one of the
most eminent European publicists of the sixteenth century,
but one of the most rational and tolerant thinkers of his time.
Yet even such a man could thus write "Of the punishments
deserved by witches":

There are two means by which states are maintained in
their weal and greatness—reward and penalty: the one for
the good, the other for the bad. And, if the distribution of
these two be faulty, nothing else is to be expected than
the inevitable ruin of the state. . . .

But those greatly err who think that penalties are established only to punish crime. I hold that this is the least of
the fruits which accrue therefrom to the state. For the
greatest and the chief is the appeasing of the wrath of God,
especially if the crime is directly against the majesty of
God, as is this one. . . . Now, if there is any means to
appease the wrath of God, to gain his blessing, to strike
awe into some by the punishment of others, to preserve
some from being infected by others, to diminish the number of evil-doers, to make secure the life of the well-
disposed, and to punish the most detestable crimes of which
the human mind can conceive, it is to punish with the
utmost rigor the witches. . . .[1] Now, it is not within the

* *Ibid.,* vol. III, pp. 5-6.
[1] Bodin then proceeds to enumerate fifteen distinct crimes, all
    horrid, of which every witch is guilty, and argues that, in
    default of proof, violent presumption should suffice for the
    sentence of witches to death.

power of princes to pardon a crime which the law of God punishes with the penalty of death—such as are the crimes of witches. Moreover, princes do gravely insult God in pardoning such horrible crimes committed directly against his majesty, seeing that the pettiest prince avenges with death insults against himself. Those too who let the witches escape, or who do not punish them with the utmost rigor, may rest assured that they will be abandoned by God to the mercy of the witches. And the country which shall tolerate this will be scourged with pestilences, famines, and wars; and those which shall take vengeance on the witches will be blessed by him and will make his anger to cease. Therefore it is that one accused of being a witch ought never to be fully acquitted and set free unless the calumny of the accuser is clearer than the sun, inasmuch as the proof of such crimes is so obscure and so difficult that not one witch in a million would be accused or punished if the procedure were governed by the ordinary rules. . . .

D.
The Philosophy of Giordano Bruno*

Dialogue I, Part i

Theme 1. Sense-perception must be interpreted by reason.

Theme 2. The universe is infinite. There is no proof of a boundary.

Theme 3. The universe is infinite because a finite world could not be self-contained and could not be imagined without position.

Theme 4. Quotes Lucretius: "If the universe is finite, what is beyond?"

Theme 5. The difficulty of defining position of a finite world in infinite space.

Theme 6. A finite universe requires the conception of a Void.

Theme 7. The space containing our universe would be

* Dorothy W. Singer, *Giordano Bruno: His Life and Thought* (New York: Henry Schuman, 1950), pp. 103-4.

void but for it. Therefore the space beyond is as our space; and in both is eternal action.

Theme 8. Sense-perception suggests rather than denies infinity (quoting Lucretius); so does reason.

Theme 9. Infinite space is the only possible conception to our minds, and can only be denied verbally, not with our thought.

Theme 10. "It is well" that this world exists—therefore also that an infinity of other worlds exists.

Theme 11. The virtue [*Bonta*] of this world cannot be communicated to another world.

Theme 12. Since we accept individual all-embracing infinity [i.e., God], no reason and no sense-perception will fail to admit also corporeal and extended infinity.

Theme 13. Our little surrounding space is as nothing to infinity and can have no relation to it; but as "it is well" that our space exists, so also is it for countless others.

Theme 14. Infinite power must act on the infinite, on infinite corporeal being.

Theme 15. Only an infinite universe can comprehend all perfection.

Theme 16 [partially repeating Theme 14]. Infinite Efficient Cause must produce infinite Effect.

Theme 17. An infinite universe is satisfying to our mind and the contrary brings difficulties and inconveniences—and we repeat Themes 2 and 3.

Theme 18. If our universe be spherical, then the space beyond it which adjoins it must also be spherical.

Theme 19. Elaborates the discussion of Theme 2.

Theme 20. Elaborates the discussion of Theme 10.

E.
The Political Theory of Francisco Suarez*

With respect to human laws, indeed, of whatsoever order, the reason [supporting the conclusion set forth in Section

* Francisco Suarez, *Selections from Three Works*, translated by G. L. Williams, A. Brown, J. Waldron (Oxford: at the Clarendon Press, 1944), vol. II, pp. 92-93.

2] may be inferred from the essential condition of law discussed in the preceding [chapter]. For just as laws are imposed upon a community, so should they be made principally for the good of that community, since otherwise, they would be inordinate. This is true because it would be contrary to every consideration of rectitude that the common good should be subordinated to the private good, or the whole accommodated to a part for the sake of the latter; and therefore, since law is made for a community, it should of its very nature be directed primarily to the good of the community.

Again, an excellent argument may be deduced in connexion with the ends [of law]. For ends should be in due proportion to acts, and to the original principles of and faculties pertaining to those acts; but law is the common rule of moral operations; consequently, the first principle of moral operations should also be the first principle of law; but their final end—that is to say, happiness—is the first principle of moral operations, since in moral matters the end to be attained is the principle of action, so that the final end is [also] the first principle of such acts; and the common good, or happiness of the state, is the final end of that state, in its own sphere; hence, this common good should be the first principle of [human] law; and therefore, law should exist for the sake of the common good. This reasoning is very nearly the same as the reasoning of St. Thomas (I.-II, qu. 90, art. 2); and it finds excellent illustration through the teachings of St. Augustine, where (*On the City of God,* Bk. XIX, chap. xvi) he infers from the due relationship of the part to the whole, and of one household to the state (of which, as he says, [the household] is the beginning or minute element), that domestic peace is related to civil peace. And he adds: 'Thus it is that the paterfamilias ought to derive from the law of the state, those precepts by means of which he so governs his household that it accords with the civil peace.' And therefore—so Augustine holds—it is far more obligatory that the laws of state should serve the common peace and the good of the state.

Another reason is clearly to be derived from the origin of

human law. For the governing power that resides in men flows either immediately from God, as in the case of spiritual power, or immediately from men themselves, as in the case of purely temporal power; but, in both instances, this power has been primarily given for the general good of the community; and therefore, that good should be held in view, in the process of lawmaking.

The truth of the minor premiss in so far as relates to the first statement, on spiritual power, is evident from the Scriptures: since it is for this very reason that Prelates are called shepherds (who should lay down their lives for their sheep), stewards (not masters), and ministers of God (not primary causes); consequently, they are bound to conform to the divine purpose, in the exercise of such power; but the principal purpose toward which God works, is the common good of men themselves; therefore His ministers also are bound to serve this end; and accordingly, the Scriptures rebuke with the utmost severity those persons who abuse that power for their private advantage. When, on the other hand, the power has been granted directly by men themselves, it is most evident that it has been granted not for the advantage of the prince but for the common good of those who have conferred it; and for this reason, kings are called the ministers of the state. It is to be noted that they are also the ministers of God, according to a passage in *Romans* (Chap. xiii [, vv. 4, 6]), and these words from the *Book of Wisdom* (Chap. vi [, v. 5]): 'Because being ministers of his kingdom,' &c. . . . Therefore, they should use that power for the good of the state, from which and for the sake of which they have received it. Thus it is that Basil (Homily XII: *On Proverbs,* at the beginning [No. 2, near end]) has rightly said that a tyrant differs from a king in this respect, namely, that the former in his rule seeks after his own advantage, the latter, after the common advantage. Aristotle (*Ethics,* Bk. VIII, chap. x and *Politics,* Bk. III, chap. v [chap. vii = p. 1279 A B]) writes to the same effect; and St. Thomas (II.-II, qu. 42, art. 2, ad 3 and *De Regimine Principum,* Bk. III, chap. xi) agrees with this view.

Now the first consequent is proved by the fact that one

of the principal acts of the power in question is law. For law is (so to speak) an instrument by means of which the prince exercises a moral influence upon the state, in order that he may govern it; and therefore, law should serve the common good of that same state.

F.
The Political Theory of Jean Bodin*

Many have been led astray by confusing the laws of the prince with covenants entered into by him. This confusion has led some to call these covenants contractual laws. This is the term used in Aragon when the king issues an ordinance upon the petition of the Estates, and in return receives some aid or subsidy. It is claimed that he is strictly bound by these laws, even though he is not by any of his other enactments. It is however admitted that he may override even these when the purpose of their enactment no longer holds. All this is true enough, and well-founded in reason and authority. But no bribe or oath is required to bind a sovereign prince to keep a law which is in the interests of his subjects. The bare word of a prince should be as sacred as a divine pronouncement. It loses its force if he is ill-thought of as one who cannot be trusted except under oath, nor relied on to keep a promise unless paid to do so. Nevertheless it remains true in principle that the sovereign prince can set aside the laws which he has promised or sworn to observe, if they no longer satisfy the requirements of justice, and he may do this without the consent of his subjects. It should however be added that the abrogation must be express and explicit in its reference, and not just in the form of a general repudiation. But if on the other hand there is no just cause for breaking a law which the prince has promised to keep, the prince ought not to do so, and indeed cannot contravene it, though he is not bound to the same extent by the promises and covenants of his predecessors unless he succeeds by strict hereditary right.

* Jean Bodin, *Six Books of the Commonwealth*, translated by M. J. Tooley (Oxford: B. Blackwell, 1955), pp. 30-33.

A law and a covenant must therefore not be confused. A law proceeds from him who has sovereign power, and by it he binds the subject to obedience, but cannot bind himself. A covenant is a mutual undertaking between a prince and his subjects, equally binding on both parties, and neither can contravene it to the prejudice of the other, without his consent. The prince has no greater privilege than the subject in this matter. But in the case of laws, a prince is no longer bound by his promise to keep them when they cease to satisfy the claims of justice. Subjects however must keep their engagements to one another in all circumstances, unless the prince releases them from such obligations. Sovereign princes are not bound by oath to keep the laws of their predecessors. If they are so bound, they are not properly speaking sovereign. . . .

The constitutional laws of the realm, especially those that concern the king's estate being, like the salic law, annexed and united to the Crown, cannot be infringed by the prince. Should he do so, his successor can always annul any act prejudicial to the traditional form of the monarchy,[1] since on this is founded and sustained his very claim to sovereign majesty. . . .

As for laws relating to the subject, whether general or particular, which do not involve any question of the constitution, it has always been usual only to change them with the concurrence of the three estates, either assembled in the States-General of the whole of France, or in each bailliwick separately. Not that the king is bound to take their advice, or debarred from acting in a way quite contrary to what they wish, if his acts are based on justice and natural reason. At the same time the majesty of the prince is most fully manifested in the assembly of the three estates of the whole realm, humbly petitioning and supplicating him, without any power of commanding or determining, or any right to a deliberative voice. Only that which it pleases the prince to assent to or dissent from, to command or to forbid, has the force of law and is embodied in his edict or ordinance.

Those who have written books about the duties of magis-

---

[1] The term used is 'lois royales'.

trates and such like matters[2] are in error in maintaining that the authority of the Estates is superior to that of the prince. Such doctrines serve only to encourage subjects to resist their sovereign rulers. Besides, such views bear no relation to the facts, except when the king is in captivity, lunatic or a minor. If he were normally subject to the Estates, he would be neither a prince nor a sovereign, and the commonwealth would not be a kingdom or a monarchy, but a pure aristocracy where authority is shared equally between the members of the ruling class. . . .

Although in the Parliaments of the kingdom of England, which meet every three years, all three orders use great freedom of speech, as is characteristic of northern peoples, they still must proceed by petitions and supplications . . . Moreover Parliaments in England can only assemble, as in this kingdom and in Spain, under letters patent expressly summoning them in the king's name. This is sufficient proof that Parliaments have no independent power of considering, commanding or determining, seeing that they can neither assemble nor adjourn without express royal command . . . It may be objected that no extraordinary taxes or subsidies can be imposed without the agreement and consent of Parliament. King Edward I agreed to this principle in the Great Charter, which is always appealed to by the people against the claims of the king. But I hold that in this matter no other king has any more right than has the King of England, since it is not within the competence of any prince in the world to levy taxes at will on his people, or seize the goods of another arbitrarily, as Philippe de Comines very wisely argued at the Estates at Tours, as we may read in his *Memoirs*.[3]

[2] A reference to Théodore Béza, *Du droit des Magistrats*, 1576?
[3] These Estates met in 1484 after the death of Louis XI. Despite the opportunity offered by the dispute over the regency, the only matter pressed by them was a reduction of the *tailles* to the lower scale of the times of Charles VII. Though concessions were made to this effect, the government made no surrender in principle of its absolute control of finance. The stand made by de Comines earned him dismissal from office and five years' imprisonment.

We must agree then that the sovereignty of the king is in no wise qualified or diminished by the existence of Estates. On the contrary his majesty appears more illustrious when formally recognized by his assembled subjects, even though in such assemblies princes, not wishing to fall out with their people, agree to many things which they would not have consented to, unless urged by the petitions, prayers, and just complaints of a people burdened by grievances unknown to the prince. After all, he depends for his information on the eyes and ears and reports of others.

From all this it is clear that the principal mark of sovereign majesty and absolute power is the right to impose laws generally on all subjects regardless of their consent . . . And if it is expedient that if he is to govern his state well, a sovereign prince must be above the law, it is even more expedient that the ruling class in an aristocracy should be so, and inevitable in a popular state. A monarch in a kingdom is set apart from his subjects, and the ruling class from the people in an aristocracy. There are therefore in each case two parties, those that rule on the one hand, and those that are ruled on the other. This is the cause of the disputes about sovereignty that arise in them, but cannot in a popular state . . . There the people, rulers and ruled, form a single body and so cannot bind themselves by their own laws. . . .

When edicts are ratified by Estates or Parlements, it is for the purpose of securing obedience to them, and not because otherwise a sovereign prince could not validly make law. As Theodosius said with reference to the consent of the Senate, 'it is not a matter of necessity but of expediency.' He also remarked that it was most becoming in a sovereign prince to keep his own laws, for this is what makes him feared and respected by his subjects, whereas nothing so undermines his authority as contempt for them. As a Roman Senator observed 'it is more foolish and ill-judged to break your own laws than those of another.'

BIBLIOGRAPHY

I. GENERAL WORKS ON THE REFORMATION

BAINTON, ROLAND H., *The Reformation of the Sixteenth Century* (Boston, 1952).

BEARD, CHARLES, *The Reformation of the Sixteenth Century in Its Relation to Modern Thought and Knowledge* (New York, 1927).

BLAYNEY, IDA W., *The Age of Luther; the Spirit of Renaissance-humanism and the Reformation* (New York, 1957).

DURANT, WILL(IAM J.), *The Reformation*. Vol. 6 of his *Story of Civilization* (New York, 1957).

FLICK, A. C., *The Decline of the Medieval Church* (London, 1930). Two vols.

GRIMM, HAROLD J., *The Era of the Reformation* (New York, 1954).

HARBISON, E. H., *The Age of the Reformation* (Ithaca, N.Y., 1955).

HOLBORN, HAJO, *Ulrich von Hutten and the German Reformation* (London, 1937).

LATOURETTE, K. S., *A History of Christianity* (New York, 1953).

LINDSAY, THOMAS M., *A History of the Reformation* (New York, 1928). Two vols.

LUCAS, HENRY S., *The Renaissance and the Reformation* (New York, 1934).

McGIFFERT, A. C., *Protestant Thought before Kant* (New York, 1911).

PAYNE, E. A., *The Anabaptists of the Sixteenth Century* (London, 1949).

POWICKE, SIR F. M., *The Reformation in England* (London, 1941).

SMITH, PRESERVED, *The Age of the Reformation* (New York, 1920).

——, *A History of Modern Culture* (New York, 1929). Two vols.

TAYLOR, H. O., *Thought and Expression in the Sixteenth Century* (New York, 1920). Two vols.

WALKER, WILLISTON, *History of the Christian Church* (New York, 1952).

WEBER, MAX, *The Protestant Ethic and the Spirit of Capitalism* (New York, 1930).

II. FORERUNNERS OF THE REFORMATION

BETT, HENRY, *Nicholas of Cusa* (London, 1932).

HUIZINGA, JOHN, *Erasmus and the Age of Reformation* (New York, 1957). A Harper Torchbook.

HYMA, ALBERT, *The Christian Renaissance; a History of the "Devotio Moderna"* (Grand Rapids, Mich., 1924).

JACOB, E. F., *Essays in the Conciliar Epoch* (Manchester, 1953).

JONES, R. M., *The Spiritual Reformers of the Sixteenth and Seventeenth Centuries* (New York, 1914).

MCDONNELL, E. W., *The Beguines and Beghards in Medieval Culture* (New Brunswick, N.J., 1954).

SPINKA, MATTHEW, *Advocates of Reform, from Wyclif to Erasmus* (Philadelphia, 1953).

STAPLETON, THOMAS, *The Life and Illustrious Martyrdom of Sir Thomas More* (London, 1928).

III. THE CATHOLIC REFORMATION

BOEHMER, HEINRICH, *The Jesuits* (Philadelphia, 1928).

BROWN, G. K., *Italy and the Reformation to 1550* (New York, 1933).

CAMPBELL, T. J., *The Jesuits, 1534-1921* (New York, 1921).

CHURCH, F. C., *The Italian Reformers, 1534-1564* (New York, 1932).

CORBETT, J. A., *The Papacy: A Brief History* (Princeton, 1956). An Anvil Book.

CREIGHTON, MANDELL, *History of the Papacy during the Reformation* (London, 1882). Five vols.

CUTHBERT, FATHER, *The Capuchins, a Contribution to the History of the Counter-Reformation* (New York, 1929). Two vols.

FROUDE, J. A., *Lectures on the Council of Trent* (New York, 1896).

HUGHES, PHILIP, *The Church in Crisis: A History of the General Councils, 325-1870* (Garden City, N.Y., 1960).

JANELLE, PIERRE, *The Catholic Reformation* (Milwaukee, 1949).

KIDD, B. J., *The Counter Reformation, 1550-1600* (New York, 1933).

PASTOR, LUDWIG, *History of the Popes* (St. Louis, 1898). Fourteen vols.

RANKE, LEOPOLD VON, *History of the Popes* (London, 1853-56). Three vols.

SEDGWICK, H. D., *Ignatius Loyola* (New York, 1923).

VAN DYKE, PAUL, *Ignatius Loyola, the Founder of the Jesuits* (New York, 1926).

IV. POLITICAL ASPECTS OF THE REFORMATION

BRANDI, KARL, *The Emperor Charles V: The Growth and Destiny of a Man and of a World Empire* (New York, 1940).

GRANT, A. J., *The Huguenots* (London, 1934).

HUME, M. A. S., *Life of Philip II of Spain* (New York, 1899).

PALM, F. C., *Calvinism and the Religious Wars* (New York, 1932).

———, *Politics and Religion in Sixteenth Century France* (New York, 1927).

V. RESULTS OF THE REFORMATION

ALLEN, J. W., *Political Thought in the Sixteenth Century* (London, 1951).

FIGGIS, JOHN N., *Studies of Political Thought from Gerson to Grotius, 1414-1625* (Cambridge, 1923).

HEARNSHAW, F. J. C., ed., *The Social and Political Ideas of Some Great Thinkers of the Renaissance and the Reformation* (London, 1925).

———, *The Social and Political Ideas of Some Great Thinkers of the Sixteenth and Seventeenth Centuries* (London, 1926).

JÁSZI, OSCAR, and Lewis, John D., *Against the Tyrant: The Tradition and Theory of Tyrannicide* (Glencoe, Ill., 1957).

LEA, H. C., *History of the Inquisition in the Middle Ages* (New York, 1888). Three vols.

———, *History of the Inquisition in Spain* (New York, 1906). Four vols.

MURRAY, ROBERT H., *The Political Consequences of the Reformation* (London, 1926).

ROBERTSON, J. M., *A Short History of Free Thought* (London, 1914). Two vols.

INDEX

VAN NOSTRAND ANVIL BOOKS already published